KITCHEN DESIGN

with COOKING IN MIND

Donald E. Silvers, CKD
CERTIFIED KITCHEN DESIGNER

NMI Publishers
Tarzana, California

Third Printing
Revised Edition 2003

Published by
NMI Publishers
18345 Ventura Boulevard,
Suite 314
Tarzana, CA 91356

Illustrations by John Reister
Photography by Ken Henry

Library of Congress Catalog Number: 93-87773

ISNB: 0-932767-09-5

Printed in the United State of America

ACKNOWLEDGEMENTS

I would like to thank the following people:

Jerry Zerg, for encouraging me to write.

B. Lesie Hart, for publishing my first article.

Carol Lamkins, Mike Goldberg, Don O'Connor,
David Andrews, my daughter Michelle, and my cousins
Essie and Diane, for the first read through
of this book and for their most thoughtful comments.

Josh Silvers, my son, who keeps me focused on the cooking process.

John Avram, for teaching me about kitchen cabinets.

NKBA dealers, for implementing my designs.
Bob Sellinger, for always responding to my frenetic phone calls
and for giving me the information I needed.

Joe Lavitt, for the title of the book.

Susan Volpe, for her patience and energy in helping me put the book together.

My editors, Louise Damberg and Carol Crotta,
for their quest to make this book the best it can be.

John Reister, for his wonderful illustrations.

My wife, Sally, who created the environment essential for this book to happen.

Special thanks to my publisher, Jerry Newmark, for
his encouragement and guidance throughout this entire project.

Moorea Hoffman, for helping edit the revised edition and who someday will
be Kitchen Design with Cooking in Mind.

Diane, for spending the time proofing the revised edition.

Melody Shapoory, for coordinating the kitchen shoots.

Ken Henry, for the great photography of the kitchen.

Mary Murphy, for her consultation.

David, for his hard work in the printing of this book.

CONTENTS

INTRODUCTION

You are about to embark on one of the most daunting experiences you'll ever have as a homeowner designing (or redesigning) your kitchen. You're no expert in kitchen design, so it is no wonder you're apprehensive. You feel as though you're at the mercy of your designer, your architect, your contractor, and your cabinetmaker. Adding to that stress is the fact you're about to invest a considerable amount of money and you will have to live with the results. You pray you will get a kitchen that not only looks good but works well.

Any number of books and magazines on the market today can tell you how to put together an attractive kitchen. Aesthetics are important, of course, but for people who cook, aesthetics are only half the story. This book tells the other half–how to design your kitchen for cooking.

Designing for the Cook

When people tell me, "I hate to cook," I've learned from experience that many really are saying, "I hate to cook in my kitchen." After you've read this book and the new kitchen is done, I want you to be able to say, "I love to cook in my kitchen." After all the money and effort, you deserve a beautiful kitchen that is also a joy to work in.

It begins with the designer. One of the most prevalent misconceptions I hear is that you don't need to understand the process of cooking to design a proper kitchen. Rarely, if ever, is a designer asked if he or she knows how to cook. And yet, the kitchen is a complex space–so complex, in fact, that it deserves the services of a specialist. The problem is that most people have spent years adjusting and re-adjusting themselves and their recipes to accommodate their kitchen's poor design. They lose sight of the potential a well designed kitchen offers. Years ago, a restaurant owner asked me to design his kitchen. After spending many weeks conferring with each employee and working at every station myself, I presented my design. Everyone loved it except the executive chef. He couldn't tell me exactly what was wrong. He simply said it didn't look right. I understood what was wrong.

This man had spent his entire 30 year career in this kitchen, working his way up from dishwasher to executive chef. He knew every nook and cranny. He felt comfortable in that environment. The changes I proposed had scared him. I asked if I could work next to him for the next few hours to show him why I had designed it the way I had. He agreed. I taped the new plan to the kitchen hood and we went at it.

While we worked, I explained to him that his kitchen actually hampered his ability to cook. The restaurant did a big business in steaks, but his refrigerator sat 20 feet from the charbroiler. The salad prep table was located right in the middle of the hot cooking area. The road to the dishwashing area wound through the cooking zone. What I proposed to do, I told him, was to consolidate his equipment and reconfigure the relationship of each one to the other.

I wanted to put in a modular charbroiler and to sit it atop a lowboy refrigerator with drawers that could hold, what else? Steaks. I rearranged the order to place the cooktop and tilting fry-pan stations together. Those had previously been separated by the deep-fat fryers. To this lineup I added another essential–a rolling steam table with a tall electric holding oven that could house several prime rib slabs, another restaurant specialty. Previously, the holding oven was 20 to 25 feet away and could only house one prime rib at a time. Additionally, I explained to the chef how I would reposition the salad table to a cooler side of the room and, also, reroute the busboys with their trays of dirty dishes.

Two hours later and with a big grin, the chef pronounced the plan great. He thanked me for showing him that, because of the kitchen's existing design, an hour's worth of work was taking him two hours to accomplish.

Most of us are like that chef. We spend our lives in kitchens that are familiar and comfortable, yet waste a good bit of our time with their inefficiency. The process of designing a kitchen must go hand in hand with a thorough understanding of the process of cooking. Only then can you achieve a kitchen that is a pleasure to cook in and that cooks well.

How Bad Design Can Affect Your Life in the Kitchen

The best example I can give that demonstrates how the design of your kitchen can affect your life is by way of a recipe. You've decided to host a dinner party for eight. The entree you've chosen to prepare is mango chutney chicken. The recipe reads as follows:

8 chicken breasts (skinned and trimmed)

Flour for dredging chicken

1/2 cup dry white wine

2 oz. orange liqueur

16 oz. mango chutney

(since chutney consistencies vary, you want to have extra on hand)

Wine or chicken stock (approx. 2 to 3 cups)

Pepper to taste

Preheat oven to 425 degrees. Cover the bottom of a 13 inch frying pan with a thin layer of rice bran oil and heat over a high flame until the oil is very hot. Dredge the breasts in flour, place in pan and fry over the high flame until browned on one side. Turn the breasts over and lower the heat. Add the wine and simmer until the liquid is reduced by half. Add the liqueur and ignite, agitating the pan as the alcohol burns off. Again reduce the liquid by half. Continue simmering the breasts until they are two-thirds cooked. Remove from the frying pan and place on an oven rack set in a broiler pan. Pour mango chutney into the frying pan and heat over a low flame, adding wine or chicken stock as needed to achieve a medium consistency. (Keep in mind that the flour residue will thicken the sauce; it should be just thick enough to stay on the breast.) When the sauce is heated thoroughly, ladle a small amount over each breast, keeping the remainder warm to spoon over the chicken before serving. Pour either the remaining wine or chicken stock (or water, in a pinch) into the bottom of the broiler pan to prevent the breasts from drying out. Reduce oven heat to 375 degrees (oven heat diminishes about one degree per second when the door is open, which is why you always want to preheat your oven about 50 degrees higher than the recommended cooking temperature) and bake breasts for 15 minutes. Place on a warm platter. Spoon the remaining sauce over the top and serve.

Now that you've read the recipe, you realize you can't make the dish in your kitchen exactly the way it is written. If you have the average stove, your burners are simply too small to properly heat a 13 inch frying pan. You might consider using three separate pans to accommodate all the breasts but give it up because the burners are too close together. You might consider frying the breasts in three separate batches, but that plan seems like too much work, and the breasts might dry out. The only other way is to use the oven. Now the process has to change. The chicken breasts must be raw when placed on the oven rack. You must spoon the sauce over them, but the sauce, too, is altered. There are no pan drippings in it now so it has lost a good bit of flavor, and it is thinner since there is no flour to thicken it. You need to bake the breasts for 25 to 30 minutes. Sounds simple, maybe easier? You're right but the chicken doesn't taste as good. Pan frying gives the flour-dredged chicken a crunchy surface, while keeping the breasts tender and soft on the inside. The textured surface also helps hold the sauce in place. In addition, the chicken breasts have a far more beautiful color when pan fried, thanks to the liqueur's glazing effect.

For anyone who cares about cooking and about eating well, these differences in appearance, taste, texture and smell are painfully apparent. I don't mean to suggest this is the only way to cook. I do believe, however, that you should have this option. Your kitchen should be filled with options and, most important, should respond to your specific needs.

Slivers' Law of Kitchen Design

How do you get the kitchen you want? You get it by beginning to explore your needs and desires, by asking yourself and then your designer a variety of questions. What kind of questions am I talking about? They deal with the basics:

- What size kitchen do I need and want?
- How many people do I cook for daily?
- How many people do I want to cook for on an informal basis? On a formal basis?
- Will my kitchen work in tandem with the number of people my dining room seats?
- What kind of appliances do I want? Do I need?
- Do I want to make structural changes?
- Do I want the kitchen to open to other rooms?
- Do I want more windows or other sources of natural light?
- Am I happy with the existing lighting?

• Do I want more or less counter and/or storage space?

• What style of decor do I prefer? What materials does it require?

• Is my kitchen in keeping with the size of my house?

• How do I prioritize my budget?

Only when you've started to consider these issues can you begin to communicate your needs successfully to your designer. Twenty-five years ago, as food director for a large charity organization, I was forced to learn the basic principles of kitchen design. I was responsible for creating 4,000 to 6,000 meals per day in a kitchen designed to generate 500 meals. To make matters even more difficult, during my first two years there, 90 percent of the food was donated on a daily basis, so a planned menu was impossible. I was in serious trouble.

Many architects contacted by the organization volunteered their help. I received more than a dozen plans to redesign the kitchen. Despite having answered hundreds of questions put to me by the architects, none of the proposals seemed adequate. It became clear to me that, since none of the architects cooked, none of them actually understood how to make this kitchen work. As I rejected one plan after another, they threw up their hands in despair. Finally, the organization's director told me to design the kitchen myself. I was petrified. "I'm not a designer, I'm a chef!" I told him. "You know what you want and what you don't want," he replied.

Fortunately for me, the noted architect/philosopher Buckminster Fuller happened to be visiting. The director asked him to see me. "Bucky" found me knee-deep in a kitchen brimming with stacked boxes, crates, and bags. As we stood in the last available two square feet of empty space, I explained my dilemma to him. He responded by asking me the following question: "How do you take space and make it usable for small or large numbers of people?" He began to talk about how a space flows and on how many levels it can flow. Since there obviously was no room to expand horizontally, he started me thinking about expanding vertically. The two floors below the kitchen lay empty and unused. I decided to turn the lowest level into cold storage space for low frequency items. The floor just below the kitchen opened to the street. I decided to turn that into the fresh food storage and prep area, and I installed a conveyor setup that allowed crates to be rolled into the kitchen from the sidewalk outside.

Essentially, Bucky taught me to break down functions in the kitchen, give those functions the necessary space, and make sure those spaces worked not only on their own but in relation to one another. The advice has served me well not only as a chef but as a designer. It has helped me to develop a principle of kitchen design that I've used ever since. Call it "Silvers' Law:"

A functional kitchen has the ability to take a given space
and expand or compress the capacity of that space
so it can respond to a given need at a given time.

In the following pages, I endeavor to reduce a complex process to its simple components in order to help you gain a kitchen that is as functional as it is beautiful. I have purposely not mentioned brand names. It doesn't matter who makes a product as long as it satisfies your needs. However, to know if it does, you must understand the product's structure, what it will or will not do, and how it will fit in your kitchen and the life you lead there.

What you want is a kitchen that is beautiful and that you can cook in beautifully. It's not the impossible dream; it's what you deserve to have.

Notes

DESIGN BASICS

I like to say that your bedroom may be the most private intimate room in your house, but the kitchen is the most public intimate room. An intimate environment is one that allows you to have a heart-to-heart talk with someone–a place where you can spend quality time with another individual. More often than not, that experience happens in the kitchen. Everything about that room–color, texture, overall atmosphere–should be inviting. Comfort is the key, and comfort comes from a number of elements. First of all, does it appeal to your senses? Do you feel good just being in the room? Additionally, comfort comes from feeling good when you're working there and by having everything you need close at hand when you need it.

Simple concepts, right? The complexity comes from the wide array of activities that occur in a kitchen. A kitchen has to work well from the morning's first cup of coffee to the 2 A.M. refrigerator's raid. It must adapt to the unique demands each activity makes on the space, whether that activity is accommodating the perpetual motion of children before, during and after meal preparation, creating a soothing haven for an afternoon cup of tea with a close friend, or graciously hosting family and guests for a meal.

Real comfort comes not just from pretty, comfortable surroundings, but from a solid, functional foundation. Comfort is knowing you can create a dinner for one, or for 20 with ease.

Any kitchen "worth its salt" should function and feel like a well designed workshop. It should offer intelligent traffic flow patterns, a smartly organized layout and all the appropriate tools. The best kitchens marry workshop efficiency to a warm, personal, attractive environment. When any of these elements is missing, the kitchen ceases to be comfortable and cooking becomes just plain hard work.

Your Kitchen as Your Workshop

If you start thinking about your kitchen as a workshop, you immediately begin to make new demands on its design. First and foremost, it must be utilitarian. It must be designed to allow you to accomplish specific tasks as simply and quickly as possible. For example, in one kitchen I worked on, it was a chore just to have a bowl of cereal. The cereal was 22 feet away from the refrigerator, and the silverware was 10 feet in another direction. In your kitchen, you should be able to bake a soufflé as easily as you toss a salad or create a wonderful sauce. It also should be flexible enough to accommodate a variety of work demands and uses throughout the day and night.

In a workshop kitchen, tools and appliances should be accessible. The more equipment that is tucked away, the more time it takes to set up and the more difficult it is to get to work. I know that some people prefer appliance "garages" or enclosed countertop cabinets that hide appliances until they are called into service. Personally, I don't, although I have incorporated them successfully in a number of designs. A kitchen is for cooking. It's only fitting that the tools of the trade be openly displayed–celebrated, if you like.

When there's not a pot or utensil in view, the kitchen becomes sterile and antiseptic. Gone is the feeling that here is where someone actually produces a meal for the family. Gleaming pots and appliances can impart a sense of warmth and well-being to a kitchen and, even, encourage more use. Displaying your tools shows your own highly personal work patterns and habits. The mood created is inviting and, yes, even intimate.

Breaking Free of the Kitchen Triangle

A good kitchen, as I've noted, is one that is instantly adaptable to different needs and can work as efficiently cooking for one as for the maximum number of people you want to entertain. Most homeowners face an immediate obstacle–the kitchen triangle. What is the kitchen triangle? You won't find it in Webster's. You will find it in most American homes, however. For decades, it has been the great bane of sensible kitchen design. The concept first emerged from a 1950s University of Illinois study that attempted to formulate the best use of small residential space for four person families. Researchers developed an approach to kitchen design that established the three major appliances–refrigerator, sink, and cooktop– as the critical three points in the kitchen, with everything else built around them.

The refrigerator was placed at one end of the space, the cooktop at the opposite end, and the sink somewhere in the middle. (The oven was simply put wherever space allowed.) It did not matter that having these three important stations at distant points in the triangle might create some inconveniences for anyone actually cooking. On paper, it looked neat and tidy and geometric. The triangle concept of kitchen design was quickly picked up by the kitchen design industry. It was an easy way to train young kitchen designers, and it crept into home after home.

There is a basic problem with the triangle, aside from the inconvenient distances. The design is static. With a major appliance located at one of three fixed points, the kitchen physically cannot compress or expand to accommodate lesser or greater amounts of food or numbers of guests. The triangle can't adjust to additional people working in the kitchen at the same time since there are no options for extending the workspace. Yet, as we all know, the kitchen serves an ever-fluctuating number of people every day. The triangle ties the cook's hands. *It is the cook who must adapt to the environment, not the environment to the cook.*

Appliances Drive the Design

Do yourself a favor and get the notion of the kitchen triangle out of your mind entirely. Instead, think in terms of flow. Good flow is the ability to cook for 2, 4, or 10 people without having to walk more than a few steps in any direction, no matter how large your kitchen is. Most kitchens are designed for a minimum number of people, not the maximum, and that's the mistake. *Always design for the maximum, not the minimum*. With proper flow patterns, you can actually double your workspace without breaking down a wall.

Think also in terms of the tools with which you need to cook. The options today are so much greater than they were in the 1950s, thanks to the virtual revolution in appliances. A range was once the sole hot cooking spot in the kitchen. Today, we speak in terms of cook-tops and ovens, toaster ovens, microwaves, convection ovens and combination microwave/convection ovens. Those aren't even the exotic options now available, such as built-in grills, deep fryers, woks and steamers.

Is it any surprise that when I'm asked what the most important element of kitchen design is, I answer, "Appliances, appliances, and more appliances?" Few people realize that poor appliances can render a magnificent kitchen nonfunctional when cooking for more than four. So, a point I cannot stress enough: *The limitations of your equipment determine the menu for the life of your kitchen*.

When you are designing your kitchen, keep in mind not only what appliances you need, but how they will be used. A microwave oven, for example, should be placed next to the refrigerator, since most of what you cook in a microwave comes directly from the refrigerator or freezer. Adding a second sink (one for prep work and the other for clean-up) becomes a must, to both break the triangle and give the space versatility. The two sink design, when spaced properly, splits the workload and allows for separate flow patterns.

This splitting of functions is liberating if you can see the possibilities. They will allow you to break free of the kitchen triangle and to create new spatial relationships. (See illustrations A through D, pages 11-14.)

To show you more exactly what I mean, let's say you are about to cook a dinner for eight. Your menu consists of a lettuce, tomato and mushroom salad with balsamic-cilantro vinaigrette dressing, pan-fried chicken piccata, zucchini with roasted peppers and walnuts and new potatoes with roasted garlic, onions, and fresh rosemary in olive oil.

You start preparing the red potatoes first since they take the longest to cook. You have to wash the potatoes, peel and wash the garlic and onions and wash the rosemary. You have now used the sink three times.

Next comes the salad, which really ties up your sink. You wash, maybe, two kinds of lettuce and then the tomatoes. If you don't have a second sink, no one else can help and you clearly can't prepare the chicken or the zucchini until you have finished those other tasks.

Now you are making the dressing for the salad and you need to use the food processor or blender or, at the very least, a jar to combine the cilantro, olive oil, vinegar, and other seasonings. In the meantime, you have roasted your potatoes, your garlic and your onions, so now you have those pans to contend with. And you haven't even gotten to the zucchini which will take another pan, the roasted peppers and walnuts which will require yet another oven tray, or the chicken which will require one or two frying pans.

In short order, it is clear that the sink will be sky-high with oven pans, frying pans, a salad spinner, a strainer, and the various utensils you've used.

The big question now is, "What do you do with the dinner dishes?" Wouldn't a second sink be nice? You might say that this menu is too much work. Yet, not one of these dishes is difficult unto themselves. With a second, well placed sink, regardless of whether or not you are the type of cook who cleans up as you go, this menu would be a snap.

If you're thinking that your kitchen is simply too small to accommodate a second sink, look at the illustrations starting on the next page. They prove that you can break the kitchen triangle in virtually any size kitchen.

This is just one example of ideas I'll deal with more thoroughly in later chapters. The basic point for now, is this: Most of us deliberately simplify our menus because our kitchens don't allow us any options. The ability to sauté, steam and grill at the same time is (we think) impossible, so typically we limit ourselves to the most ubiquitous of menus–*e.g.*, a salad made in the sink, a roast with baked potatoes in the oven, a vegetable cooked on top of the stove and a dessert either bought or made in advance. Anything more interesting or complex demands so much extra labor due to the inadequacies of our kitchen layouts and our appliances that we don't usually attempt it. If we do, we start cooking Saturday's dinner on Wednesday. The true joy of making such a meal is thus diminished or missing altogether.

The Subsystem Approach

As rational human beings, we derive great pleasure from creating order out of chaos. We try to break down a process to a series of steps. We try to develop a system.

Think of the kitchen as just such a system–*i.e.*, one demanding order but flexible enough to be versatile. Think of cooking as a process that must be broken down step by step. Each step corresponds to, and makes use of, a part of the kitchen system. Each of those parts are subsystems of the overall kitchen design. If you can imagine designing your kitchen with an understanding of the cooking process and the subsystems involved, you will not only have gained valuable insight into cooking itself but will very likely end up with a kitchen that responds beautifully to your cooking needs.

Sound a bit confusing? Let's run through the stages of cooking a meal to demonstrate what I mean. Pretend it's that moment when you walk into your kitchen to plan a meal for 12. You begin thinking about your guests, their tastes, the time of year, whether it's brunch, lunch, or dinner and how elaborate an effort you want to make. Planning is part of the whole process.

The first subsystem is where you plan the meal: a kitchen desk area with bookshelves to house all your cookbooks, notepads, pens, perhaps a log book of past successful menus and a telephone.

Then, once you've shopped, you need other subsystems–*i.e.*, adequate unloading and storage space for both dry and cold groceries. Planning, storage, food preparation, cooking, clean-up–all of these are subsystems. If any one of them is missing or not functional, the process breaks down. The result for you is harder work, longer time in the kitchen, potential chaos and a lot less enjoyment.

In the following chapters, we'll take a look at each of these subsystems, how to make efficient use of them, and how to avoid common design pitfalls.

TYPICAL KITCHEN TRIANGLE

BREAKING THE KITCHEN TRIANGLE

ILLUSTRATION A

BEFORE

AFTER

ILLUSTRATION B

156" (13'-0")

177" (14'-8")

DW   SINK

RANGE

REF

BEFORE

ILLUSTRATION C

156" (13'-0")

177" (14'-8")

OVEN

MICRO

DW

CLEAN UP SINK

POTS & PANS

BREAKFAST ROOM

CUSTOM HOOD

POTS & PANS

RANGE

DIRTY DISHES

PREP SINK

FOOD FLOW OUT

FOOD FLOW OUT

CHAR BROILER

FOOD FLOW OUT

DIRTY DISHES

REF

DINING ROOM

AFTER

14

174" (14'-6")

108" (8'-6")

60" (5'-0")

RANGE

SINK

REF

BEFORE

ILLUSTRATION D

174" (14'-6")

170" (14'-2")

BREAKFAST ROOM

PASS THRU

PANTRY

DINING ROOM

DIRTY DISHES

FOOD FLOW OUT

DIRTY DISHES

CLEAN UP SINK

PREP SINK

DW

REF

POTS & PANS

FOOD FLOW OUT

FOOD FLOW OUT

CHAR BROILER

COOKTOP

HIGH BTU COOKTOP

DOUBLE OVEN

AFTER

Notes

Notes

STORAGE SUBSYSTEMS

The first element in good kitchen design is the storage subsystem. By storage, I mean both dry storage, or cabinetry (which holds everything from plates, pots, pans, utensils and dry and non-refrigerated foodstuffs) and cold storage, or the refrigerator/freezer (which maintains the perishables.)

Cabinetry Dry Storage

When you walk into a kitchen, your first impression most likely comes from its cabinetry. It's usually the most dominant feature and tends to set the tone aesthetically. Cabinetry can also dominate a kitchen design budget. It generally represents between 25 and 50 percent of a kitchen's total cost.

As important as it is, both in terms of style and function, cabinetry often presents a formidable obstacle to good kitchen design. In a properly designed kitchen, it is the appliances that drive the design, and the cabinets work to support appliance placement. But the cabinet industry has long set the standards when it comes to dimensions. In a sort of tail-wagging-the-dog situation, manufacturers create appliances to fit into the cabinet industry's standardized 22 inch deep European to 24 inch deep American cabinets. Stop for a moment and consider the consequences: Cooktops are designed to fit a cabinet, not to address whether you cook for 2, 6, 12, or 20 people.

This problem can often be addressed by having your cabinetry custom built, which is a pricey but worthwhile expense. While you'd have a hard time customizing a stove, oven, or sink, you can and should get exactly what you want and need in your cabinetry.

Where do you begin? A local cabinet shop? A home improvement center? A furniture store? A kitchen showroom? A contractor? An architect or designer? The process can make your head spin. I find that, for most of my clients, the best way to begin is to decide which period or style you like–*e.g.*, country, Shaker, contemporary and so on. You will begin to get a picture in your mind of what your kitchen will look like. Then, sit down and figure out realistically how much storage you need. (See questionaire on page 84.) Then decide how much money you can spend.

However, be generous with your estimate. Keep in mind that your cabinets are the resting place for everything in your kitchen. If you choose poorly, or short change yourself, you won't be able to extract those cabinets without ripping out the countertop, disconnecting the appliances, and almost certainly ruining both your floor and walls. If properly designed and constructed, your kitchen cabinets will outlive you. Now is your chance to do it right. But what is right?

☐ Your options

Roll-out shelves, spice drawers, pull-out pantries, pantries of varying depths, vegetable drawers, built-in lazy Susans, wine racks, tilt-out wastebaskets, built-in cutlery dividers, tray partitions, lid storage racks, tray and cookie sheet storage racks, and door racks for packaged foods are just some of the options that today's innovative cabinetry designs offer. (See illustration E, page 19.) Each can make your life infinitely easier. For example, with the usual pot and pan storage cabinet, you oftentimes end up on your hands and knees to find the one pan you need that is sitting at the very back of the cupboard. A simple roll-out shelf pulls straight out of the cabinet to fully expose everything on it.

There are basically four types of cabinetry on the market today: stock modular, semi-custom modular, custom modular and custom millwork. Let's look at them one at a time, from the least to the most expensive.

Stock modular. You've seen it at your local lumberyard, home improvement center, or kitchen warehouse. Stock cabinetry, which is pre-manufactured and sold right off the floor, is most frequently used by builders, contractors, and do-it-yourselfers. As the least expensive type available, stock cabinetry offers few options. You may be able to choose between two door styles, one to three finishes and limited sizes and configurations.

Most 24 inch or 30 inch wide wall and base cabinets of this type have a stile, or post, running vertically through the center of the cabinet's interior for structural support. Stiles are inconvenient in that you must reach around them to retrieve items. Another drawback to stock cabinetry is that you will end up designing your kitchen around the cabinets, rather than having the cabinets conform to your needs. Unless you're really pressed for dollars, I wouldn't consider that option.

Semi-custom modular. If money is a problem and anything custom is out of reach, I would consider semi-custom modular cabinetry an acceptable option. These lines are a cut above plain stock cabinetry in that they offer a greater variety of sizes and styles. Rather than one or two door choices, you may have a dozen to choose from. The selection of stains and laminates with different finishes is more diverse. Unlike stock cabinetry, which can be purchased straight off the shelf, semi-custom modular cabinetry must be ordered. But don't deceive yourself, you still must essentially design your kitchen around these cabinets.

Custom modular. Most companies offer custom modular cabinets in 3 inch increments, up to 36 inches in frameless and 48 inches in framed. However, you can customize these cabinets to measure any size. You can also order angled or rounded (known in the trade as radiused) cabinets. Some brands of custom modular cabinets can be ordered elaborately carved or hand-distressed for an aged look. Some lines are very high quality, a fact reflected in the moderate-to-high price tag. But they are well worth it.

ILLUSTRATION E

SPICE DRAWER INSERT

KNIFE DRAWER INSERT

PULL OUT CHOPPING BLOCK

PULL OUT IRONING BOARD

TILT DOWN DRAWER FRONT

PULL OUT TOWEL BAR

STAINLESS STEEL BREAD BOX

MIXER LIFT

VEGETABLE BINS

PULL OUT TABLE

PULL OUT COUNTER

PULL OUT PANTRY BASE

CAN STORAGE DOOR RACK

PULL OUT TRASH CAN

DOUBLE PULL OUT TRASH CAN

Custom millwork. A good local cabinetmaker can create a kitchen to your exact needs and specifications. There are many positives to ordering custom millwork. For one, the craftsman is right there in front of you, able to make adjustments or correct mistakes as you request.

The major advantage, of course, is that custom millwork (as well as custom modular) cabinetry serves, and does not dictate, the overall kitchen design. The big negative is that a local cabinetmaker will not be able to give your cabinets any finish that is as good as the catalytic conversion-varnish finish that custom modular cabinets feature. (This finish is explained on page 23.)

Choosing cabinetry

Most people don't realize that the cost of cabinetry generally relates to how the door is made, what the door style is, and what type of wood or laminate is used. Twenty feet of cabinetry may cost $10,000 if the door is plain. But give the door a simple raised panel and the price jumps to between $12,000 and $14,000. A raised panel door requiring multiple moldings and a good deal of manual labor may run $20,000. Add angles or rounded edges and you could be looking at $25,000 to $30,000. If you want the door in a formed polyester, you're at $60,000.

Although there are many cabinet door styles, there are only two kinds of cabinet "boxes": framed and frameless. A framed cabinet features a vertical member, or stile, and a horizontal member, or rail. The hinges attach to the stile, and the box comes with either an inset door which sits flush with the frame, or an overlay door which sits on top of the frame. A frameless cabinet has no stiles or rails. It is simply a box with hinges placed inside. (See illustration F, page 21.)

There are differences between the two that go beyond how they look. For example, if you want a frameless angled, double-access, or sink cabinet, it will have to be strengthened. Frameless cabinets can also cost you more because of their size. You can specify a 48 inch framed cabinet, but you generally don't want to go beyond a 36 inch frameless cabinet, because it is not structurally sound. So if you choose frameless cabinets, you may need more of them.

American base cabinets run 34-1/2 inches high. The toe kick is 4 inches high by 3 inches deep. European cabinet manufacturers make their toe kicks 6 to 9 inches high in order to line up with the standard 36 inch high American counter and American appliances. You need to know these differences in sizes because, if you choose European cabinetry, you will lose 2 to 5 inches of cabinet storage space. In a small kitchen, inches count. (See illustration G, page 22.)

Of course, there are many cabinet manufacturers and a wide range of cabinets to choose from. Given the same kitchen design, you can find yourself with bids anywhere from $10,000 to $80,000. The difference in price reflects the materials used, the intricacy of the craftsmanship, the quality of the hinges, whether the drawers pull out completely or only

CABINET CONSTRUCTION

FRAMELESS   FRAMED

TALL CABINET

WALL CABINET

BASE CABINET

ILLUSTRATION F

DIFFERENT HEIGHT TOEKICKS

4" TOEKICK

6" TOEKICK

9" TOEKICK

ILLUSTRATION G

three-quarters of the way, the amount of customizing you desire, and the uniqueness of the style. Whatever you choose, be sure to have the measuring and installation done by your cabinet provider, rather than your own carpenter or contractor. That way, if there are any problems, they won't become yours and you will know where to point your finger.

Materials and finishes. Most cabinets are made of oak, maple, pine, or birch. Other more exotic and rare woods, such as cherry and walnut, will cost you more. Particleboard, which ranges from low grade sawdust to high grade compressed wood slivers, is often covered with a laminate or resin soaked sheets of paper pressed together to form a veneer. The thicker the laminate, the stronger and more durable the cabinet will be.

Given a cabinet of decent quality, the finish determines its durability. Wood furniture can take any number of finishes, such as paint, colored lacquer, polyurethane, oil or varnish. Kitchen cabinetry, however, because of its exposure to moisture, grease, and grime, stands up best with a baked-on catalytic-conversion varnish. Nothing on the market today holds up as well. Not only does this finish make your cabinet impervious to kitchen wear and tear, it is nearly maintenance free. The one problem with this finish is that it is generally only available on modular cabinetry and is usually beyond the facilities of your local custom cabinetmaker. A good way to test whether your cabinets can stand the test of time is to dab a hidden spot with some acetone or nail polish remover. If the finish stands up to it, the cabinet is likely to be impervious to household chemicals and cleansers, marking pens, food stains and most other common kitchen threats as well.

Refrigeration Cold Storage

Cold food storage is, essentially, no different than dry food storage. Refrigerator manufacturers like to have you think in terms of cubic feet. Resist. Think instead in terms of shelf space. By doing so, you'll be much better able to assess your needs and find the appliance that addresses those needs.

When you shop for a refrigerator, you will have a choice of side-by-side (refrigerator on right side, freezer on left), over-under (freezer on top, refrigerator below) and under-over (refrigerator on top, freezer below), in sizes that include 24", 27", 30", 36", 42" and 48". (See illustration H, page 24.)

Most people use a refrigerator far more than they do a freezer. The general rule is that a person goes to the refrigerator between 17 and 21 times more often than they go to the freezer. The over-under is therefore the least useful model as you must bend constantly to retrieve anything. Even though it is the most energy efficient model on the market (it may save you $20 a year on your electric bill), think about the human energy it wastes. However, if the choice is between a 36 inch side by side or an over-under with a 36 inch freezer on the bottom, take the over-under. The alleged convenience and larger capacity of a 36 inch side-by-side is wasted since the freezer takes up disproportionate space for its frequency of use. Vital refrigerator space has been sacrificed and the result is a refrigerator incapable of

DIFFERENT REFRIGERATORS

36" OVER-UNDER

48" SIDE BY SIDE

32" UNDER-OVER

36" ALL REFRIGERATOR

36" SIDE BY SIDE

48" SIDE BY SIDE
WITH ICE AND WATER
DISPENSER

36" THREE DOOR
WITH ICE AND WATER
DISPENSER

36" ALL FREEZER

42" SIDE BY SIDE

36" OVER-UNDER
CAFE DOORS

ILLUSTRATION H

accommodating a number of bowls or platters of food prepared ahead of time for a party.

Single door refrigerators can be hinged to open either right or left, depending on your space. Refrigerator doors on side by sides, whether the 36 inch, 42 inch, or 48 inch model, hinge only on the right. Thus, in designing with a side-by-side in mind, both the sink and the countertop must be to the left or you will constantly have to walk around your refrigerator door to put anything down. Picture yourself reaching into such a refrigerator and pulling out a quart of milk in one hand and a plate of butter in the other. How do you shut the door? Your choices are to use your foot or your backside. This bears repeating: Placing the sink and countertop to the left of a side-by-side is essential.

There is a new animal bridging the gap between freestanding and built-in refrigerators. It is the counter depth freestanding refrigerator. Like a typical freestanding, it is 68 to 72 inches tall and comes in fridge top, freezer top, and side by side configurations. But unlike a standard model, the counter depth freestanding is, as it's name implies, designed to line up with your cabinets and counters. This means that it is 24 inches deep at the box or case of the refrigerator, with the door adding another 2-1/2 to 3 inches of depth. Since many standard refrigerators are 36 inches deep, this is a considerable difference. Currently, counter depth models are more expensive than their standard depth equivalents and they offer less capacity. If you want a shallow profile but need more storage than a 36 inch can provide, look to the 42 and 48 inch built-in refrigerators.

With the advent of under-counter refrigeration, any combination of 24 inch wide refrigerator and/or 24 inch wide freezer units can be specified. Refrigeration options can multiply by installing more units where they add to convenience. The small size of those units allows them to fit into unusual or simply small places.

There are also refrigerator and freezer drawers. Those are 27 inches wide and work beautifully as additions to standard refrigerators. Imagine the flexibility and efficiency of storing produce at the prep island, drinks and snacks in the family room and frozen meats in the pantry. The choices are endless and this type of flexibility is important in large kitchens where point-of-use storage is critical in streamlining the cooking process.

Some people like the look of commercial refrigerators. These models come in a variety of sizes. They are all in stainless steel, some with stainless steel doors and others with glass doors. Glass doors, while attractive, don't offer many benefits. For instance, you can't have shelves on the door. Certain models also have a depth of only 24 inches, though some make up for the loss of space in height–e.g., 84 inches versus the standard 64 to 67 inches. These shallower units do have the advantage of lining up with the standard base cabinets so the refrigerator doesn't jut out into the room. And gone are the days when you would find a container at the very back of a shelf containing a green substance that was once tomato sauce. With 24 inch deep refrigerators, all food items are at your fingertips.

A final note on refrigeration: Ideal internal temperature should range between 36 and 40 degrees Fahrenheit. Most manufacturers achieve zone temperatures and humidity control through drawers and other closures for butter, cold cuts, vegetables and fruits. Tomatoes will thrive best in the butter area, where the temperature is around 50 to 60 degrees. Fish and shellfish will do best in the back of the refrigerator, where the temperature is a few degrees colder because it is less effected by the opening and closing of the door. If you have any concerns about your refrigerator's temperature setting, buy two or three temperature gauges so you can test its different dial settings in different locations.

FOOD PREPARATION SUBSYSTEMS

Good preparation space means that everything you need is within two or three steps. That includes your food processor and other small appliances, your cooktop, oven, pots and pans and prep sink. But the single most important element of a good food preparation system is lots and lots of counter space.

Counters

One of the biggest problems most clients articulate to me concerns kitchen counter space: There simply isn't enough of it, or it's in the wrong place. They are right. As far as I'm concerned, most kitchens do not have enough counter space, and it is in the wrong place. Several culprits are to blame. The kitchen triangle is one. The sink, stove and refrigerator positions dictate where the counters end up, not where counter space is actually needed. A more basic problem can be traced back to the building practices of the '20s and '30s and, more specifically, to the ubiquitous 4 feet by 8 feet plywood sheet. Back then, it was customary to set studs 16 inches apart. It was also customary to create 8 feet ceiling heights. The 4 feet by 8 feet plywood panel conveniently spanned floor to ceiling and three studs. That piece of plywood also determined the size of the wall and base cabinets. A contractor could simply order the panels in bulk, use some for walls, then slice the remainder down to create counters and cabinets. So, in most older houses, base cabinets measure 22 inches deep and wall cabinets 12 inches, creating a 22 inch deep counter.

None of this did much to promote efficient function in the kitchen. It was all a matter of convenience and economics for the builder. Base cabinet depths were later modified to 24 inches to accommodate the built-in dishwasher. To my mind, however, the 24 inch deep counter still isn't deep enough for most kitchen work. Not only is there no space to lay things out, it becomes impractical to leave out the small appliances you need to have handy for food preparation. If you do keep them out on the counter, you have no room to work. You're forced to labor vertically rather than horizontally.

What do I mean by "vertically" and "horizontally?" It's natural and optimally efficient for us to spread out our work so that everything is easy to see and easy to reach. When we don't have enough horizontal or side-to-side space, we start to work vertically. In other words, we stack. Containers are placed on top of containers; utensils and packages are placed on top of refrigerators or ranges or in sinks, or anywhere we can find space. Does this sound painfully familiar? There is salvation, however. It comes in the form of the 30 inch deep counter.

☐ The 30 inch Deep Counter

When I began to consider what a cook truly needs to prepare food properly, I thought how nice it would be to take cold food from the refrigerator, a roast from the oven and vegetables from the range all at the same time and still have space for the small appliances that have been employed to make these dishes. All this can be accomplished with a 30 inch deep counter. How do you get such a marvel? There's no real mystery. You simply set the traditional 24 inch deep base cabinets six inches away from the wall and extend the counter back to the wall. This process is called "furring out" the cabinets. To answer the question I know you're about to ask, I say, "Yes, you can see a 6 inch space from the side." That's not a problem–just be sure to order a 30 inch deep side panel and the space will never show.

If you have any doubt about what a wonderful work surface the 30 inch deep counter creates, see illustration I, page 29. Notice how much counter space there is, even with the small appliances sitting at the back of the countertop. With such a design, your food preparation surface is working for you, not against you.

☐ Counter surfaces

There are five basic counter surfaces. I'll go over them from the least to the most expensive.

Post-formed and custom laminates. Decorative laminates are created much like puff pastry, layer upon layer. The process uses different kinds of papers, soaked in resin, then pressed together using about 1,200 pounds of pressure at a temperature of 280 degrees Fahrenheit. Laminate makes an excellent surface, both aesthetically and functionally. It resists scuffs and stains, and its smooth surface is easy to clean and maintain. Post-formed or prefabricated laminates and custom laminates are made the same way. The difference between the two are design options and price, with custom running about double the price per square foot as the post-formed. The relatively inexpensive price tag of laminates is their main attraction, as well as the fact they have no grout lines to collect dirt and stains. On the other hand, should you scorch, burn, or cut a laminate surface, you'll need to replace the whole piece.

Ceramic kitchen tile. Kitchen tile, a traditional and reliable choice, offers you an extraordinary range of options in terms of colors, patterns, and sizes–everything from 4 inches by 4 inches to 12 inches by 12 inches and up. I prefer to use a minimum of 6 inch by 6 inch tiles because they minimize the number of grout lines, while offering a range of design options. Tile will take hot pots and can be combined successfully with other interesting materials, such as granite or solid surfaces. However, you do end up with the dreaded grout lines. In a contemporary pattern, the grout lines can be butt joints as thin as 1/16 of an inch. In a rustic, country style design, however, the tiles should feature large grout lines of 3/16 inch or 1/4 inch, clearly a case of form over function.

While it is easy to be dazzled by the variety, there are important questions to ask. Will this tile hold up on a kitchen counter? High-gloss tile, for example, does not stand the test

25 1/2"
11" 14 1/2"

STANDARD
24" DEEP
CABINET

24"

30"
11" 19"

STANDARD
24" DEEP
CABINET
PULLED 4 1/2"
OFF WALL

4 1/2" 24"

248" (20'-8")

BROOMS

WASHER/DRYER
BEHIND DOORS

PANTRY

114" (9'-6")

PREP SINK

36" COMMERCIAL
TYPE RANGE (30" DEEP)

REF

MICRO

CLEAN UP SINK   DW

18"

30"

54"

18"

30"

ILLUSTRATION I

of time because the finish will dull and scratches will show. A better choice is a matte finish. Another question: Are trim pieces available in this pattern? The edge of your counter requires a curved piece of trim called a bullnose or V-cap; the counter corner needs inside or outside corner pieces and the sink also needs corner pieces.

You may want to mix tiles to your personal taste, but this can be problematic since tiles vary in length and width as well as in depth. If you do want to mix them, I strongly advise you to hire the best tile setter you can find or you may end up with an expensive disaster.

Wood. Wood is certainly a beautiful material. If the counter is built from hard maple butcher block, it will provide a smooth, durable surface you can use a knife on. There are real problems with wood, though. It requires heavy maintenance. It should be bathed in mineral oil every three months to prevent it from drying out and cracking. It can also scorch, burn and stain easily. And wood carries a moderate to expensive price tag.

Solid surfaces. Solid surfaces generally are composed of resins, polyesters, and/or acrylics. The mix depends on the manufacturer, who usually trademarks the name. Regardless of which product you choose, solid surfaces are wonderful because they take abuse better than any other counter surface. Solid surfaces are nonporous and resist staining and burning. Also, since the color runs equally through the entire piece, you can repair minor bum marks and scratches by rubbing it with steel wool or 320 to 400 grit sandpaper. On the down side, solid surfaces cannot take a hot pot and they expensive.

Granite. With its range of colors, granite is one of the most exciting and dominating materials in kitchen design today. Its surface is like glass, it cleans easily, is hard to stain if sealed properly, and will take a hot pan. Granite is, however, one of the most expensive surfaces you can use. It can also overpower your kitchen design aesthetically. Quartzite is in the same family and has the same characteristics as granite.

After reading this list, I'll bet you want to know which one I recommend. I'll sidestep answering that by saying your choice should depend on your personal taste and on your budget. All of the surfaces will, in fact, function quite well, especially with the use of trivets and cutting boards.

Small Appliances

Whether your kitchen is tiny or spacious, tools and equipment that you use daily should be literally at your fingertips, in order to save you time and energy. The problem arises when you have a kitchen with limited counter space and you must keep the countertop clear of appliance clutter in order to work. If you have adequate depth, however, you can store your appliances at the back of the counter. Make sure your backsplash, or the covering between the top of the counter and the bottom of the wall cabinets, is at least 15 to 18 inches high. If you have sufficient cabinet storage–and you're tall enough–I would recommend the 18 inch height. This means the bottom shelf of the cabinet will be four feet, seven inches from the floor.

Consolidating small appliances can go a long way toward maximizing what counter space you do have. By consolidating, I don't mean gathering them all together in one spot; I'm talking about consolidating functions. For example, a mixer, blender and standard food processor can all be replaced by a more powerful, versatile food processor, which can cut, chop, blend, whip, knead, slice, strain, shred, julienne and pureé–in essence, it can do everything those other appliances do. The many accessories for these new processors can be neatly housed in a drawer. The processor itself can be stored on a pull-out shelf that swings up and locks into place at, or just below, counter height. Food processors can handle about 90 percent of all prep work, although cooks who do a lot of baking may feel they need a heavy-duty mixer as well.

Another space-saving option is appliances that attach to the underside of wall cabinets, effectively lifting them off the counter entirely. These include can openers, coffee makers, some small microwaves and knife sharpeners which come in cordless and plug-in varieties.

Built-in food centers are motors set directly into the counter that attach to a food processor, blender, or other appliance. They are worth considering for small kitchens with minimal counter space. These machines can mix, blend, grind coffee, crush ice and perform a dozen tasks in a compact space. While food centers are helpful in a small kitchen, they are actually a liability in a large kitchen, since they are stationary and thus limit work flow. For large kitchens, I recommend appliances that can be moved from here to there.

The new kid on the block is the immersion blender. It looks like a stick with blades at one end and a handle at the other, attached to a long cord and plug. This strange beast is called a blender, but it actually is a blender/hand mixer hybrid. Not only can the two speed immersion blender accomplish everything the blender can, it can also whip cream and beat egg whites into peaks. The cord makes it portable so you can, if you choose, pureé a sauce right in the cookpot. It is small, easy to clean, and can hang from a bracket fastened to the counter backsplash to relieve counter clutter. As far as I'm concerned, the immersion blender is one of the most efficient pieces of equipment to hit the marketplace in a long time. My two pieces of advice for its use: Employ tall pots because it can spatter and always start on low speed, then move to high for thorough mixing.

The Appendix includes an appliance frequency survey designed to help you figure out your cooking patterns and needs. Use it!

The Prep Sink and Other Prep Areas

The counter is the main, but not the only, preparation area to consider when designing or redesigning your kitchen. A little creativity, combined with common sense, can gain you both extra space and efficiency.

Take, for example, the notion I spoke about earlier, the second sink. I will talk about the specifications of sinks more fully in Chapter 5, Clean-Up Subsystems, but I can't pass up another opportunity to lobby for the addition of a second sink in the kitchen. This second sink, as I've mentioned, is largely the cook's sink, to use for food preparation, while the first sink functions almost solely for clean-up chores, or as a second prep area when you are preparing for a large party. A second sink is just the type of utility station that can break the kitchen triangle, split the workload, and create separate flow patterns for the different tasks each handles. As such, it is well worth the cost. Make sure dirty dishes can travel directly from the table to the clean-up area without crossing the path of the prep area. Also, if the distance between the prep sink and the clean-up sink is too great, you may want to consider a dishwasher for the prep area as well.

For a preparation sink, I recommend a single, deep bowl. It should be a minimum of 16 inches wide, although I prefer 24 inches because I clean my pots and pans as I work. A good prep sink must be deep enough to handle your biggest pots and whatever rinsing, soaking and washing tasks are at hand. The prep sink should be either tile-in, which means flush with the counter tile, or under-mounted, in which case the sink sits below the counter surface, so that food scraps can be easily swept from counter to basin.

This is not the only helpful food prep option. Another one I like a great deal is the rolling table. A kitchen needs to be a minimum of 12 feet wide to accommodate a 24 inch deep island, which even at that only allows for a 3 foot wide aisleway. So if you don't have a 12 to 14 foot wide kitchen, you can still very effectively extend your counter space by using what is actually a type of rolling island. The rolling table can be used as a stationary unit and fitted with an overhead rack to hold pots and pans. If it has a drawer and a lower shelf, you end up with additional storage space. (See illustration J, page 33.)

The rolling table's best feature is its mobility. It can roll from the refrigerator to the sink or the range as needed for actual cooking or food preparation. When covered with a tablecloth, it turns into a movable buffet that can be rolled straight into the dining room for service. Then it can roll right back into the kitchen with the dirty dishes for clean-up.

The rolling table offers the type of flexibility that makes a kitchen an effective workplace, since it allows you the freedom to redefine your work space as you need it. Rolling tables come in a variety of surface area sizes, from 18 inch by 18 inch, up to 2-1/2 feet by 5 feet. Any size larger may present mobility problems. In other words, you need to make sure it can pass through the doorway between your kitchen and dining room.

Other prep area helpers include an inset stone slab for pastry rolling. Use granite, not marble, since marble is very porous and can stain and spot easily. All counter materials, with the exception of butcher block, dull knives, so it is critical you cut on a wood cutting board. Set it next to the sink, so scraps can be easily swept away. Make sure you reserve a wide drawer in the prep area for your utensils and a cupboard for your bowls and measuring cups. All of these ideas will speed along your prep process and cut down the energy you need to get the job done.

ROLLING TABLE

HOOKS ON ENDS
FOR POTS & PANS

ILLUSTRATION J

Notes

COOKING SUBSYSTEMS

As I've mentioned, inadequate counter space forces a cook to work vertically rather than horizontally. A poorly designed cooktop will victimize you in the same way. If your burners are small and close together, you must use smaller, taller pots, which require you to constantly stir the contents so the food at the bottom doesn't burn and the food at the top isn't undercooked. Think about it, how many recipes have you read requiring top of the stove cooking that you realized you couldn't prepare because your burners were inadequate?

Cooktops

Generally speaking, the four factors to consider when buying a cooktop are the number of burners, the distance between the burners, the adequacy of the heat and the efficiency. Having said this, I must add that almost none of the standard American or European cooktops work particularly well. As a whole, they are poorly designed. The burners are not large enough, they do not emit enough heat and they are badly placed in relationship to one another. (See illustration K, page 36.)

Cooktop manufacturers have not kept pace with today's cooks. Take sautéing, which requires large front burners that give off high heat. You would think manufacturers would place them where they belong. Unfortunately, that's not the case. Most cooktops have one small and one large burner in front; others have two small burners in front and the larger burners in back.

Those configurations made some sense at one time, when a small front burner was needed to melt butter or to do other tasks requiring a small pan and a low flame. But today, microwave ovens take care of those kinds of jobs faster and better. What we now need from our cooktops are larger burners with better control–burners that can handle a 13 inch pan when cooking for large groups and that can quickly switch from high heat for sautéing to low heat for poaching.

One of the most important considerations for any cook purchasing a cooktop is the strange term "recovery ratio." Recovery ratio, in the commercial kitchen world, means the amount of time it takes for the fat or liquid in a pan to get back to the temperature it reached before adding the food to be cooked. Think of making pasta. You bring the water to a rapid boil, then add the pasta. The recovery ratio is the amount of time it takes for the water to again come to a boil. The lag time matters less for boiling pasta than it does for, say, pan frying, when you start by heating some type of oil or butter and then add the poultry, fish or meat. Immediately, the oil or fat loses much of its heat. The slower the recovery ratio of your

DIFFERENT STANDARD COOKTOPS

36" FOUR BURNER GAS COOKTOP
WITH ELECTRIC GRIDDLE/GRILL
AND DOWNDRAFT

36" FIVE BURNER GAS COOKTOP

36" FIVE BURNER GAS COOKTOP
WITH DOWNDRAFT

36" ELECTRIC COIL COOKTOP
WITH GRIDDLE/GRILL
AND DOWNDRAFT

36" FOUR BURNER
ELECTRIC HOB COOKTOP

MAGNETIC INDUCTION COOKTOP
(SHOWN TWO DIFFERENT WAYS)

30" GAS COOKTOP

ILLUSTRATION K

cooktop, the greasier your food will turn out.

Recovery ratio is linked to the amount of heat, or British Thermal Units (simply, BTUs), a gas burner generates. One BTU equals the amount of heat required to raise the temperature of one pound of water one degree Fahrenheit. In an electrically powered cooktop, energy is measured not in BTUs but in watts. Watts translate to BTUs on the order of roughly one to four: 1,000 watts equals about 4,000 BTUs. An electric cooktop's large burner, or element, generates 1,800 to 1,900 watts, which equals 7,200 to 7,600 BTUs, while small elements run 600 to 800 watts, or 2,400 to 3,200 BTUs, technically. I say "technically" because, in reality, gas cooktops lose 25 to 35 percent of their heat (unless the burner is sealed) so an electric cooktop's large element is roughly equivalent to something more like a 12,000 BTUs gas burner.

☐ Your options

I'm often asked what type of cooktop I recommend. You have basically three choices: gas, electric and magnetic induction. Gas is the most popular by far, so I'll start there.

Gas. Professional cooks use gas more than any other source of heat. Of course, they're playing in the big leagues. A burner on a professional cooktop generates between 15,000 and 25,000 BTUs. The average residential gas burner produces between 6,000 and 12,000 BTUs, and that is only on one or two of the burners. This disparity can make a significant difference in the quality of the food you're sautéing.

Have you ever asked a restaurant chef to give you the recipe for a certain dish you love, tried it at home, and it just didn't work? He insists he gave you the right recipe; you insist he must have left out a secret ingredient. What the two of you do not realize is that the key ingredient is heat!

Still and all, gas provides the home cook with the greatest number of options. You can see the size of your flame, and you can control it instantly.

Gas cooktops feature combinations of one, two, four, five, six, or eight burners and run from 30 to 48 inches wide and from 19 to 27 inches deep. As I've mentioned, you want to know the amount of BTUs the burners generate, the size of the grate that the pot or pan sits on, and the distance between the burners. You also want to know how large a pan will fit on each burner. Shopping for a cooktop becomes much easier if you take along your largest frying pan or stockpot.

There are two styles of cooktops on the marketplace today–the drop-in cooktop and the professional style cooktop, also called a range top. Drop-in cooktops are anywhere from 30 to 45 inches wide and from 19 to 21 inches deep. They are designed to fit on top of the counter and can have 4 to 6 burners. By far the most popular type is the 36 inch, five burner cooktop. The configuration of the knobs and burners varies from brand to brand. The best models put the knobs to one side so you have room to slide pots around and use 13 inch pans without being concerned that the pan will prevent you from reaching the knobs. Most of these units have one high heat burner (usually 12,000 to 15,000 BTUs) in the center with one small and one medium output burner in front and the same in back. The best units, of course, have burners that are all the same size with the ability to set the flame to a simmer or sauté temperature on every one. The drawback to this kind of unit is it's narrow depth. Twenty-one inches is small enough so that one large pot per side is about all you can manage, which makes 30 inch versions impossible to work with.

A 13 inch pan will fit nicely on rangetops. This type of cooktop features four to eight burners and is typically 30, 36, or 48 inches wide, although some are available in 60 inches. They are usually 24 to 26 inches deep and the knobs are up front, allowing for two to three more inches in depth and width of usable space. This combination will allow two decent sized pans to fit front to back, unlike a drop-in cooktop. They typically have between 15,000 and 20,000 BTUs per burner and usually all the burners have the same range from high to low, allowing the cook greater flexibility and ease. These, to me, are the most desirable cooktops available. Many clients assume they don't need a cooktop that big, that powerful, and that looks that commercial. But looks can be deceiving. Those are the only cooktops that give you all your options.

I have a couple of cautions about cooktops with sealed and heavy-duty burners that generate 12,000 BTUs and up. With some of these cooktops, simmering can be difficult without the use of a heat diffuser, or metal plate, that sits between the pan and the burner grate to lower the amount of heat transferred. Luckily, heat diffusers are inexpensive and can be found at most hardware or kitchen supply stores. Be sure to check with the cooktop manufacturer to see if you can simmer on every burner without the use of a heat diffuser. Some cooktops have a dedicated simmer burner but, again, that limits your choices.

Also, be wary of any continuous grate, oftentimes referred to as an "S" or "V" grate because of the design. Even after you have turned off the heat, the temperature will remain constant for a considerable length of time, so you need to make sure you slide the pot or pan to another area of the cooktop. That type of grate can also be dangerous to your hands, so take care!

Electric. Most electric cooktops, which generate about the same energy as gas cooktops, have all the same inherent problems–not enough heat, small element size, and not enough distance between elements. Still, some clients prefer them. They claim electric is cleaner and produces no gas fumes, which is certainly true. Electric cooktops come with two, four, five, or six elements. I recommend six, since the response time for heating and cooling electric elements is notoriously slow. In fact, the wait can drive you crazy. My advice for electric cooktop users who know they will need both high and low heat while cooking is to pre-heat two elements, one high and one low. Then simply move your pan when you need to.

Electric cooktops offer a choice of element styles–coil, hob, or flat top. Coil, a metal heating element in a spiral shape, allows you to see if the heat is on or off, since the coil turns red when hot. The slightly raised hob is opaque and usually black, which looks neat and clean, but you can't see whether the heat is on or off. Also, large pots and pans tend to trap the heat and cause the element to turn off. Flat tops, made from ceramic glass, are the worst, in my view. You can't see the heat and spillage is a real cleaning problem.

Magnetic Induction. The only type of pots or pans you can use on a magnetic induction cooktop is those made of ferrous metal–that is cast iron, steel, or triple stainless steel. Unlike traditional cooktops, magnetic induction surfaces do not have a direct heat source, such as a flame or coil. Magnetic induction works by causing the pan's metal molecules to vibrate, thus creating energy, which generates heat. The four burner cooktop itself stays cool although, after a pan is removed, you can feel the heat left by the pan's bottom.

Magnetic induction, while absolutely superb for low heat tasks–such as melting chocolate or butter, steaming, and poaching–has in the past been unable to generate enough heat to adequately sauté. Given sufficient time, a cast-iron skillet will be able to reach a sufficient temperature, but it will also stay very hot for a long time since cast iron dissipates heat relatively slowly. Thus, you lose control over your cooking process.

However, there are some new products coming on the market place that have 3,000 watts, enough to generate the kind of heat necessary to achieve a decent recovery ratio. One company is producing an induction wok which promises the equivalent of 35,000 BTUs!

With lower wattage units, by adding two gas burners, if space allows, you place them side by side with 13,000 or more BTU capacity. The average cook rarely needs more than two high heat burners. This combination of gas and magnetic induction gives you the best of both worlds–options that give you high heat and efficient low heat that is easily accessible. In addition, if the power ever goes out, you will still be able to put a meal together.

Other Cooking Surfaces and Equipment

☐ Your options

There are a few other choices and necessities you need to consider before your cooking decisions are complete.

Charbroilers. With today's emphasis on low fat cooking, charbroilers are a terrific addition to any kitchen. These units generally consist of an iron grill over simulated charcoal briquettes, with a catch pan underneath. Not only are meat and fish wonderfully tasty, but vegetables are extraordinary.

Although you can choose between gas and electric charbroilers (see illustration Q, page 40) the smart choice is gas because it offers an additional thousand degrees of heat. The flavor in grilling comes from melting fat, which hits the coals, turns to smoke, rises and adheres to the food's surface. The greater the heat, the more smoke it creates and the tastier the food.

In today's market, gas charbroilers are available as part of a larger unit. (See illustrations page 48.) They are typically combined with four burners in a 36 inch cooktop or range, or with six burners in a 48 inch cooktop or range. There is a 30 inch wide charbroiler that is separate from any cooktop on the marketplace today. Be aware that this addition to your cooking surface will require additional ventilation in your hood. Also, you should not put a shelf over the grill because the shelf will be very difficult to keep clean and could reduce the efficiency of your ventilation.

For years, I had a love/hate relationship with my gas charbroiler. I loved cooking on it

CHAR BROILERS

NEW BREED 48"
SIX BURNER GAS
RANGE WITH DOUBLE OVENS
WITH GRILL AND HIGH SHELF
BACKSPLASH

ELECTRIC

ILLUSTRATION L

but hated cleaning it. I was tempted to throw it into my self-cleaning oven, but the manufacturer's instructions said not to, lest the porcelain finish burn off the grate. Porcelain, aside from its general attractiveness, helps to prevent foods from sticking. Then one day a client of mine told me damaging the porcelain finish doesn't matter. He told me to simply brush my charbroiler with an oil that has a high burning point (such as corn oil) before using it and the food would never stick. Then the grate can be placed in a self-cleaning oven. Suddenly, clean-up became a breeze.

Griddles. A few manufacturers now show griddles with their cooktops and ranges. At first glance, it seems like a good idea. The positives are the ease with which you can cook pancakes, crepes, bacon, and sausages. However, you lose two burners in order to accommodate a griddle. Griddles also do not allow immediate adjustment of heat. They are high maintenance, requiring frequent oiling to prevent rust, and may be dangerous when there are children around since there is no visible heat source. From my point of view, the negatives far outweigh the positives. Instead, buy a griddle that fits on top of the range or cooktop burners, or buy an electric griddle that sits on the counter.

Hoods/ventilation systems. The kitchen's ventilation system is often an afterthought for many clients. In fact, ventilation is critical to the proper and healthy functioning of any kitchen. Ventilation systems should be considered as important a purchase as any other major appliance.

There are a variety of ventilating systems on the market today, including ceiling and wall fans (which are basically worthless), recirculating units (which merely move air around in the hood and back into the room), and downdraft and updraft systems. The only ventilating system that really works is an updraft unit, which requires a hood. Equipped with a blower, the system pulls smoke through a filter, then out through a duct cut into the roof or the side of the house.

Hood and ventilation systems are rated in cubic feet per minute of air movement, or CFMs. Since vapors rise, you want to make sure you have a large enough container, or plenum, to catch them all. Rather than delve into these more technical aspects, let me simply describe to you what you need.

The hood should extend three inches beyond each side of your cooktop or range, six inches on each side if you also have a charbroiler. For example, if your cooktop or range is 36 inches wide, your hood should be 42 inches wide. When there is no charbroiler the depth of the hood should be at least the depth of your range or cooktop. I prefer three inches beyond manufacturers' recommendations. Believe me, you'll never miss the six inches of cabinet space like you would miss a clean, well ventilated kitchen.

Height from the floor is unimportant if the hood has sufficient CFMs to draw all the waste. Many times I have put the bottom of the hood 72 to 76 inches off the finished floor, rather than the standard 57 to 66 inches, so that taller people can walk under the hood without banging their heads against it.

DOWNDRAFTS

POP-UP DOWNDRAFT

FIXED DOWNDRAFT

ILLUSTRATION M

I've often had people ask me why the hood doesn't pull the smoke out completely. I've suggested opening a window and, lo and behold, it works. In commercial kitchen design, we worry about pulling out pollutants and putting the air back (*i.e.,* make up air). In a residential kitchen, opening a window usually will do the trick.

On occasion, I've had to use downdraft ventilation systems which pull the smoke down and out a floor duct under the house. That is necessary when the cooktop is on an island and you don't want to use a hood because it appears too massive or if you can't vent up structurally.

In these situations, cooktops generally take one of two kinds of ventilation systems. One lies flat, centered between the burners. The other rises six to seven inches behind the cooktop. (See illustration M, page 42.) Of the two, there is no question that the latter is superior. It is elevated over the cooktop, giving it a better chance to catch pollutants. Both, however, are imperfect because they cannot capture all the rising vapors the way a plenum can.

Ovens

There has been a virtual revolution in oven design since the days of the single range oven. No longer relegated to "wherever space could be found," today's ovens can perform an array of tasks and have become integral in good kitchen design.

☐ Your options

Five types of ovens are available on the market today: the standard electric radiant oven, the convection oven (the true convection and the fan-assisted), the microwave oven and the convection/microwave oven.

Electric radiant. This oven is the one most familiar to us. It has two heating elements–one positioned at the top for broiling, and the other at the bottom for baking and roasting. In some of the newer units, both top and bottom elements can be used for baking. In the standard radiant oven, heat rises from the bottom of the oven to the top, pushing the cold air down but also creating hot and cold spots that can result in uneven cooking. We all know what it's like to put two trays of cookies on an oven's two shelves. The cookies on the bottom cook much faster than those on the top because they are closer to the bottom heating element. The trays must be reversed halfway through the baking time or the cookies on the bottom end up burnt and the cookies on the top end up undercooked. For my money, there is a better oven on the market–the convection oven.

Convection. There are actually two types of convection ovens available today: the true convection and the fan-assisted. Some domestic ovens are fan-assisted, which simply means that the manufacturer has added a fan to the back of the standard electric radiant oven. (See illustration N, page 44.) I'm not saying this type of oven isn't good, but it simply can't handle the large volume of food that a true convection oven, with its additional racks, can.

In the fan-assisted oven, the heat comes from the exposed elements at the top and bottom,

OVEN HEATING SYSTEMS

RADIANT OVEN

EXPOSED HEATING COILS

TRUE CONVECTION OVEN

HEAT SOURCE
OUTSIDE OF OVEN CAVITY

ILLUSTRATION N

with the bottom contributing 75 percent of the heat and the top contributing 25 percent. The fan circulates the heat in the oven cavity to eliminate hot and cold spots. This type of oven generally can handle only two racks of food at a time, even though the manufacturer usually provides a third rack. If you use all three racks, you will have to rotate the food at some point, because the top and bottom racks will brown faster than the middle rack due to their direct exposure to the two heating elements.

A true convection oven differs in that the heating element is wrapped around the fan, which causes the heat to flow evenly over all the racks. There are three to four racks in the oven, and you never need to change their positions, even for baking. But that's not the only benefit: In a true convection oven, you can simultaneously place a tray of cookies, a pan of fish and a pan of poultry. The aromas and flavors will not mingle because the continuous air flow prevents odors from escaping.

Convection ovens are beginning to appeal to the consumer for that reason and because they appear, from the outside at least, to be smaller. That brings me to an important point–the proper way to measure oven capacity: In a standard radiant oven with exposed heating elements, the cooking space is measured from the bottom rack to the top heating element, not from the oven floor to the ceiling.

Still, as good as it seems, a convection oven has its problems: The forced air flow can cause dryness in some foods. Adding a liquid, such as stock, wine, or water to a roasting pan helps combat the problem. But many bakers will not use convection ovens for baking such items as meringues, or anything with phyllo dough or puff pastry for just that reason.

The beauty of most convection ovens made for home use is that they can switch from convection to radiant, or radiant to convection. You have options, which, as you know by now, is my favorite word. For example, if you have a dining room that seats 10, 12, or 14 people, I would consider having a smaller convection oven on top with a larger one on the bottom. Again, don't be deceived by how tiny the small, European built-in convection oven appears. It will easily handle a 20 pound turkey. So you may want two different size ovens–a small one for daily use and a larger one when entertaining crowds.

Convection ovens are now made 36 inches wide, with the oven cavity 24 inches wide. That means the oven racks, when not in use, are too large to store anywhere in most standard kitchens. Be sure to have your designer specify a base cabinet that is 12 to 15 inches wide in order to store these racks vertically.

Microwave. Microwaves are an energy source that cook food from the outside in by agitating the water molecules in the food, which creates friction and which in turn creates heat. They are, in essence, steam machines. In microwave ovens, the most important quality to look for is wattage; your best bet is to buy the highest possible. The reason is simple: the higher the wattage, the faster the food cooks. You want to be able to cook with low, medium, or high heat in small and distinct time units.

A good microwave cookbook is a must, but be aware that there is no standardization among them. Medium in one book can mean 275 degrees and in another 325 degrees, so you will need to do some experimenting with whichever microwave you choose.

Most of my clients use their microwaves for melting butter, warming leftovers and reheating coffee. Microwaves work in tandem with refrigerators and freezers and should always be placed near them. Microwaves can fit on the counter or be built into a wall cabinet. If you are tight for space and want the microwave off the counter, there are models now that can be hung from the bottom of a wall cabinet.

If you want to fit a microwave into a tall cabinet or into a wall space, be sure to buy a trim kit or frame that secures the microwave into the cabinet or into a wall space and that has a small vent at the top to allow air to flow around the unit. If you want to put an oven into the bottom of a tall cabinet and the microwave up top, leave plenty of space between them, since the hot air rising from the oven can damage the microwave's digital pad. One last item to note: All but one manufacturer build microwave ovens that hinge only on the left, so make sure you can open your door the way that makes good sense.

Convection/microwave. I am not referring here to any type of portable countertop unit. I am talking about a full size, built-in oven, which runs roughly from 12 to 30 inches wide, 12 to 18 inches high and 15 to 20 inches deep. These ovens have the capacity to cook by microwave or convection heat or by both of the above.

These combination ovens can be of great help to the working person who likes to have a home cooked meal but does not have a lot of time in which to cook it. These ovens allow you, in most cases, to throw in a little microwave power while cooking with convection methods and they won't change the texture of the food being cooked. While a convection/microwave oven will microwave anything you put into it, don't expect it to replace your 600 to 800 watt countertop unit, which efficiently concentrates the energy in its small cavity. Food takes longer to microwave in a combination oven because the microwave energy diminishes within the larger cavity. You might say that it gets "lost in space."

Combination cooking works well with almost any baked good. An apple pie can be baked in half the time and still produce a brown, flaky crust. Most casseroles and stews also do well, but roast meats do not since microwaving essentially steams meat.

A few general closing notes on ovens: All ovens have thermostats. Manufacturers calibrate their ovens very carefully but, with common use and time, the calibrations can be off. The best way to check your oven's true temperature, if you have any doubt, is to buy an oven gauge at a kitchen supply store. If there is a discrepancy and you've had the oven less than a year, most manufacturers will come out and fix it for free.

Also, keep in mind that if you stack ovens, you lose two to two-and-a-half feet of counter space. If you can afford it, fine, but most small kitchens can't. Counter space comes under the heading of high frequency use, while ovens are low frequency. Placing both ovens under the counter may mean you'll have to bend a few times a week, but it may be worth the trade-off. It's your decision to make but ponder it carefully.

Ranges

A range is a cooktop and oven combined in the same unit, designed mainly for space savings. The average range measures 30 inches wide, which accounts for the same problems cooktops suffer: The burners are too small and don't generate enough heat.

However, a new type of range is on the market today, incorporating the new breed of cooktops which include griddle and charbroiler options. (See illustration O, page 48.) This new range looks commercial but is specifically made for the home. It is insulated so it can butt up against cabinets without scorching them, and the burners are sparked by electronic ignition. This type of range comes in a number of sizes, from 30 to 60 inches wide. Range depth is 28 to 32 inches, so make sure it doesn't project so far out as to create traffic problems.

The smaller, single oven range comes in either convection or radiant. The larger one, with two ovens, comes with one convection and one radiant oven or both radiant. The convection oven option will add dollars, but to my mind it's well worth it.

A range's big plus is that it saves high frequency use counter space. While it may be convenient to have your oven in a tall cabinet, you need to think carefully about how often you use your oven versus how often you use your counters.

Also, if you decide to invest in a range that has gas burners with high BTUs, be aware that it may require a three-quarter inch gas line instead of the standard half-inch. Be sure to check manufacturer's specifications, as they can change at any time without notification.

RANGES

NEW BREED 48"
SIX BURNER GAS
RANGE WITH DOUBLE OVENS
WITH GRILL AND HIGH SHELF
BACKSPLASH

NEW BREED 36"
SIX BURNER GAS
RANGE WITH 6" BACKSPLASH

30" FREE STANDING RANGE

30" SLIDE-IN RANGE

ILLUSTRATION O

Notes

Notes

Chapter 5

CLEANUP SUBSYSTEMS

Washing dishes, glasses, pots, pans. Cleaning produce, fish, fowl, meat. Disposing of containers, wrappings, food waste, peelings. Because this subsystem is so all-encompassing in the cooking process, it deserves as much care and planning as any other aspect of good kitchen design.

Sinks

As I'm sure you've noted by now, I believe strongly in the two sink kitchen and I don't mean the traditional two basin sink. Kitchen clean-up has evolved just as every other kitchen function has. It's time we catch up with reality.

Remember washing dishes as a kid? There was one central sink, made up of two, usually equal size, 13 inch basins. We filled one side of the sink with soapy water to wash and the other side with clear water to rinse. Today, for the most part, we use the sink to simply rinse dishes before we load them into the dishwasher. The dishwasher now performs the function of the first sink, making the 13 inch double basin sink a dinosaur.

Configuration is the most important factor in choosing a sink. I think the worst sink on the market, as you've probably already guessed, is the standard 33 inch double bowl. The two basins measure a scant 13 inches each, leaving very little room to wash larger pots and pans. However, there are a variety of double sink configurations, ranging from 33 inches to 48 inches, that work much better, even at the 33 inch dimension. (See illustration P, page 52.)

Sinks generally come in one of five materials: enameled steel, cast iron, stainless steel, quartz and solid surface material. I'm always asked which one is the best. My response is, "Which do you like?" If you buy a quality sink, it should last a lifetime regardless of the material.

Aside from solid surface sinks which are integral to the countertop itself, sinks are installed in kitchen counters in three ways: self-rimming or top-mounted, flush-mounted, and under-mounted. (See illustration P, page 52.) A self-rimming sink is the easiest to install, since it simply drops into the hole cut out of the counter. It isn't the best design, though. The rim juts up above the countertop so when you need to scrape food from the countertop into the sink, you must push those scraps up and over the rim. It's a messy, inefficient, and often unsuccessful endeavor. If you must have a self-rimming sink, be sure to buy a cutting board that rises higher than the lip so you can easily slide the scraps for easy disposal.

I prefer either a square, so-called "tile-in" sink, which sits flush with the tile, or the under-mounted rimless sink. In both of these designs, the sink sits at the same level or lower

DIFFERENT SINK CONFIGURATIONS

SINK INSTALLATIONS

SELF-RIMMING SINK

FLUSH-MOUNTED SINK

UNDER-MOUNTED SINK

ILLUSTRATION P

than the countertop, so wiping food from the counter into the sink for disposal is easy. Single kitchen sinks designed for prep work range from 15 to 24 inches wide. You don't want anything smaller than a 15 inch sink or the garbage disposal will not fit the drain hole. Let your work routine be your guide. If you wash your pots and pans as you go along, you'll want the largest sink that can fit. If not, you can go with a smaller one. My last piece of advice concerns placement. Almost every home or kitchen design magazine I pick up shows the prep sink in the middle of the island. Don't put it there. A six foot island with a one-and-a-half foot sink plunked in the middle leaves you a virtually useless two feet and change on either side. Setting the sink at one of the island's ends will gain you four-and-a-half feet of continuous counter space.

☐ Your options

All sinks come with holes drilled into their back ledges, although they can be ordered without them. The holes are to accommodate faucets, air gaps, soap dispensers and other options such as retractable spray faucets for easy clean-up of pots. A standard 33 inch porcelain or stainless steel sink will have four holes. If you need an additional one, be sure to order it. Another note: Strainers and baskets do not come with many sinks, so be sure to order them too.

Faucets. Faucets will require from one to three holes if sink-mounted. There are essentially two types of faucets: single or dual control. The single control, which requires one hole, mixes hot and cold water in one valve. The dual, which requires three holes, has separate hot and cold valves. A single lever type is the most efficient, especially for the prep sink area. When your hands are dirty or full, you can adroitly maneuver the lever with your elbow. However, single or dual control is a personal choice, depending solely on which you're more comfortable with.

When buying faucets, the price difference has to do with the quality of the metal, valves and surface covering. Some faucets include retractable sprayers; others require a separate attachment. Generally, faucets with pull out sprayers are more durable and more expensive. Some manufacturers give lifetime warranties on them.

An air gap, which uses one hole, is required in some states. Air gaps provide a break in the dishwasher drain line to prevent the drain water from siphoning back into the dishwasher. Check to see if your dishwasher comes with one.

Soap dispensers also require one hole. They consist of an under counter reservoir and above counter pump top that allows you to pump soap directly into the clean-up sink. I personally find this option indispensable.

Many people like the idea of an instant hot and cold water faucet, which requires one hole and a switch so you can flip from cold to hot. A small chiller, or refrigerator unit, in the sink cabinet provides you with water that is cold enough that you don't need ice. A booster, or small hot water tank, heats the water to flow at 190 degrees, which is hot enough for an instant cup of tea or the best filtered coffee. There is one problem with the hot water dispenser: At 190 degrees, it can burn you, so use extra caution.

Water processing systems. There are three popular water processing systems on the market today: filtration, reverse osmosis and distillation. Their main difference is the amount of minerals they are capable of extracting from your tap water.

Filtration, purchased by about 60 percent of the market, uses carbon and takes out the bad taste, but none of the minerals. Reverse osmosis, which is used by approximately 35 percent of the market, passes the water through a carbon membrane filter, removing about 95 percent or more of all the minerals. Distillation, at about 3 percent of the market, requires a booster heater, which boils water to create steam that removes 100 percent of the minerals. Your local department of water and power can inform you about these and other systems.

Disposal. Garbage disposals, powered electrically, grind up food. There are two types on the market today: continuous feed and batch feed.

With continuous feed, you flip on a switch and the disposal starts grinding. You can continually push food waste into the disposal without pausing. The danger is getting your hand caught. Some stores sell a safety unit that sits in the drain and has a flanged top that you push the food through while the water flows to the disposal through veins in the unit's side.

A batch feed is completely safe, since you push down all the food waste first. Then you insert a stopper into the disposal opening and turn it to start the motor. The negative is that, as the name suggests, you have to grind your waste in batches.

The most important factor when buying a garbage disposal is power. The greater the horsepower, the quieter it will be and the fewer problems you will ultimately encounter. It is better, for example, to purchase a three-quarter horsepower disposal than a one-half horsepower unit. There is not much difference in price and the latter, as it grows older, will more likely break down because it has had to work harder.

Buying a more powerful garbage disposal also makes a difference in warranty. The one-half horsepower model will generally come with a one year warranty, while the three-quarter horsepower carries a five year warranty.

If you choose a continuous feed disposal, make sure it features reversible stainless steel blades. These blades will reverse themselves if some material gets stuck, thus maintaining cleanliness and extending the life of the disposal. Spending the extra dollars up front means fewer dollars handed over to the plumber later.

One last piece of advice: If you are tearing up your kitchen, do not even think about reinstalling your current disposal. I cannot explain why these units become inoperable when reinstalled, but I have consistently experienced this problem over my many years as a designer.

Dishwashers

It's a complete mystery to me why domestic dishwasher manufacturers do not produce residential dishwashers that process faster than the usual 60 to 120 minutes. If you're using the pots and pans cycle, it can take as long as 140 minutes. That's right, more than two hours. There are, admittedly, several commercial under the counter dishwashers that will do the job in four minutes, but these require 240 volts versus the usual 120. They do not dry the dishes, and they are unkind to good china. Domestic American made residential machines are water guzzlers, consuming 12 to 14 gallons per load.

European dishwashers, on the other hand, are leagues ahead in both speed and water consumption. A few have fast cycles, lasting from 12 to 20 minutes. They will do a good job as long as you do not include pots and pans in the load. Dishes should air dry in a few minutes after opening the door. As far as water use goes, the frugal European machines use a mere four to five and a half gallons. They are also quieter.

Most dishwashers today will wash dishes without pre-rinsing. Food particles either collect in a trap which easily removes for cleaning, or are ground up in an internal disposal system and swept away. As a matter of fact, it is better for your dishes if you don't pre-rinse because dishwasher soap is highly alkaline. Without food residue to work on, the soap works directly on the dish surface, potentially etching it. The soap can also etch glasses and pit silverware. One of the ways you can combat this dishwasher wear and tear is to only fill the main soap compartment of the standard two. As it turns out, the water in the first rinse cycle usually isn't hot enough to dissolve the soap anyway.

Almost all dishwashers are a standard 24 inches wide, so your choice of machine will not affect your space planning. However, it will make a difference when the time comes to choose your cabinetry, since you may want the dishwasher door panel to match. If the kitchen is very large or if you throw a lot of dinner parties or have big crowds, you may also want to put in a second dishwasher in the prep area.

If you are right handed, the dishwasher belongs to the left of the sink; if you are left handed, it belongs to the right. All dishwashers come 34 to 34-1/2 inches high, so fitting them under the standard 36 inch counter is no problem. However, if you wish to lower the counter, only European models come with adjustable legs that allow the dishwasher to be raised or lowered two to three inches.

The price difference in dishwashers is related to options. The least expensive come with one wash arm, stationary racks, and a choice of two cycles. Those in the medium price range offer two wash arms, two to four cycles, a filtering system, a sanitizing cycle that reaches 140 degrees, and some insulation. The most expensive give you three wash arms, adjustable rack positions, adjustable length cycles, a separate silverware rack, a built-in air gap, a hot water booster that raises the temperature by sensor to 140 degrees plus, and, in general, far better insulation. Some even feature a built-in water softener and most are ultra-quiet.

Trash Compactors

Whenever a client requests a trash compactor, I wince. Knowing the many problems that can develop with them, I usually say, "Whoa." For starters, they create odors and attract insects and sometimes rodents, even when they are kept meticulously clean.

The idea behind trash compactors is well meaning. Squashing the trash to one-quarter its size saves precious landfill space. But times have changed. Since many cities now require that citizens recycle separate types of trash, trash compactors may have outlived their usefulness. I prefer, instead, a recycling center located behind a door in a base cabinet next to the clean-up sink. This kind of recycling center is essentially a drawer which pulls out almost completely on gliders and has two attached wastebaskets, one for bottles and cans, the other for paper and packaging trash. This system allows for fast and easy separation.

Notes

Notes

TWO CRITICAL DESIGN ELEMENTS FROM FLOOR TO CEILING

From top to bottom, the design of your kitchen is now almost complete. While flooring and lighting do not directly fit into any subsystem, they are immensely critical to the proper functioning of each one of them. Now that you have a kitchen that invites you to cook, it will do you no good if your flooring isn't easy to clean and, more important, easy on your legs and spine. It also will do you no good if your lighting doesn't allow you to determine when the food in the sauté pan is just right, much less the ability to read a recipe.

Flooring

Next to cabinetry, your flooring can dominate your kitchen's aesthetics more than anything else. Interestingly, the most expensive choices are not always the kindest to the cook, so you want to think carefully before making a decision.

☐ Your options

There are basically five different kinds of flooring surfaces. I'll discuss them in order of least to most expensive.

Vinyl sheet and custom vinyl. Vinyl sheet goods, manufactured in rolls, are simply cut to the dimensions of your floorspace and then installed as a single piece. Vinyl is easy on the feet and back and, with today's coatings, it cleans up to a shine and does not mark or yellow, unlike yesterday's linoleum. The downside is that if you drop a pot on it, the flooring will dent. Decorative choices are limited, but vinyl also comes in tile or strips.

Custom vinyl is priced and installed by the square foot, and has the same easy maintenance and easy on the body features as vinyl sheet. It comes in a wide range of colors and patterns, which can be cut in a variety of ways and then laid in an array of different patterns. Though the seams may show dirt, for the money there's probably no better choice.

Hardwood. It's beautiful, and because of its "give," it's also easy on the body. However, it is high maintenance, requiring polishing and immediate clean-up after spills. Pets and children are a terror to it.

Designer woods. Simply stated, designer woods are merely wood flooring that is covered with a clear vinyl veneer. Easy maintenance and kindness to the spine are the positives; the negatives come in its limited choice of grains and colors.

Ceramic tile. Its decorative choices and low maintenance make it a prime choice for the design oriented. However, it is very hard on the feet and back. Items dropped on it will likely break and it could chip and crack. Oil and grease spills are a particular danger since they make this surface exceptionally slick. In addition, like ceramic tile on your countertop, you will have to deal with those nasty grout lines.

Natural stone. If you want a kitchen with a rustic look, there is no more enticing choice. But standing for any length of time on a stone surface will make you feel it. If you drop something on it, the floor and/or the item may crack or break. In addition, you will still have to deal with grout lines, and stone, unlike most other materials, will stain. Marble, granite, limestone and flagstone are popular choices.

Lighting

Complexity is the key word when attempting to recommend lighting choices for the kitchen. With the myriad of different city and state codes, as well as the options offered by incandescent, halogen, fluorescent, recessed, spot and other kinds of lighting, it is almost impossible to tell you how you should light your kitchen. Instead, let me tell you where you should light it.

Lamps and fixtures under wall cabinets will light three-quarters of the counter, from the backsplash out. The color of your counter surface will reflect light, so the lighter the counter, the better the light. Your ceiling lamps and fixtures should be placed above the outer quarter of your counter so that, with your cabinet lighting, all surfaces will be lit. Finally, your overhead lighting should cast a balanced light and not leave any dark spots.

Whenever possible, try to use more than one switch for your various lighting. For example, the hood, peninsula, ceiling, under cabinet and above cabinet lights in my kitchen have separate switches and some are on dimmers. This allows me to light just the parts of the kitchen I'm working in so it is energy efficient, and it is also a great way to create different moods.

Be sure to have your electrician tell you what switches are available and what your various appliances may require. Gone are the days when a small appliance needed only 300 to 400 watts of power. Many today use 700 to 1,000 watts. You need to know if your electrical panel has enough power, and what effect your new appliances may have on your pocketbook.

Finally, wherever there is counter space without water, there should be an electrical outlet, or more if you can accommodate them. Also, have your electrician install the outlets horizontally rather than vertically so your cords don't get tangled together.

In addition, when you're redoing your electrical sections, your plumbing will be exposed, so now is the time to change all your old pipes. Never remodel without getting permits from your local city hall. Their inspectors will come to the job site to make sure the work has been done correctly and to existing codes. Then you can feel confident that you are safe and protected.

Notes

Notes

THE TOOLS OF THE TRADE

A workshop, no matter how thoughtfully or expertly planned and organized, is nothing without the right tools. Pots, pans and knives are the kitchen's basic tools. They work intimately with your preparation and cooking subsystems, yet you'd be surprised at how many clients overlook their importance.

I have had clients spend as much as $250,000 for a new kitchen, yet keep around pots and pans that should have been thrown out years ago. When I design a kitchen, one of my favorite tasks is taking the client shopping for new pots, pans, and knives, helping them understand how purchasing the right tools for their needs can make all the difference.

Pots and Pans

No question, pots and pans are a significant purchase. However, choosing the right pots and pans requires the same consideration and has the same importance as any other aspect of your new kitchen design.

Most important to understand is that the pot or pan should not control the cook. So the first order of business is to think about the tasks you will undertake with them. Do you need high, low, or sloped sides? Is the weight right for the task? For example, if you're steaming vegetables or boiling pasta, you can use inexpensive, lightweight pots. But if you're making stock, you must have a thick, somewhat heavy pot that can simmer very gently or your stock will turn dark.

There are other factors to consider. First, lids should fit tight. A tight lid is like a tightly closed oven door. It ensures that no heat or moisture escapes and it creates a mini-oven on the cooktop. The next critical element is the pot or pan handle. Does it fit your hand; does it resist heating; can it withstand oven temperatures if need be?

Wood, plastic, and assorted metals are the three basic materials for handles. A wood handle will never heat up and is easy to grip when your hands are wet or greasy. But wood can burn over a high flame and cannot go in the oven. Plastic handles have the same heat problems as wood and also tend to slip in wet or greasy hands. Metal handles often become very hot to the touch, but I use them because they easily go into the oven. Be sure you immediately empty the contents of the pot or pan after use and then place it under water to prevent damage to your counters or danger to your hands. Whatever handle material you choose, make sure it balances with the weight of the pot or pan.

Next on the list of considerations is the size of your cooktop and the spacing of its burners or elements, since they will dictate the size of your pots and pans. For example, if you have 12 inch burners, don't buy a pan larger than 13 inches.

Aside from these factors, the ability to transfer and dissipate heat are the key issues for the cook. How rapidly and evenly does heat transfer to and move through pots and pans? How quickly does heat dissipate when the heat source is turned off?

Heat conduction differs according to the type and the thickness of the construction material, and here is where most people go wrong. There is no single "right" material for all your cooking needs. That is the problem with buying pot and pan sets–they don't take into account the need for different materials for different cooking tasks.

For example, a slow cooking stew requires a pot that will absorb heat slowly, steadily, and evenly, so that the different flavors can mingle gradually while the meat stays moist. Cast iron fits this bill. Sautéing, on the other hand, demands fast and even heat transfer throughout the pan. But a sauté pan must also dissipate heat quickly. It must cool rapidly the minute it is taken off the heat source because disaster can result if it continues to cook the food at high heat. Aluminum or copper, lined with stainless steel, works best here.

☐ Materials

Let's examine some of the major pot and pan materials, their uses, advantages, and drawbacks.

Stainless steel. Stainless steel is one of the most durable materials for cooking and will not react chemically with foods. Unfortunately, stainless steel diffuses heat unevenly, causing food in different parts of a pan to cook at different rates. Also, it scorches and is difficult to clean. To perform well, stainless steel should be bonded to another metal, preferably aluminum or copper.

Cast iron. Cast iron is excellent for certain cooking tasks. It absorbs heat slowly, distributes it evenly and retains it for a long time. Cast iron works best for cooking stews, casseroles and preparations that go from the top of the range into the oven, such as a pot roast that is braised on the range top, then finished in the oven. However, the very qualities that make cast iron perfect for long, slow cooking make it unworkable for fast cooking processes, such as sautéing. Cast iron also rusts easily and requires careful cleaning, thorough drying and some maintenance. The unfinished, porous surface of a cast iron pan must be "seasoned" before the first use and dried very carefully after it is washed in order to prevent rusting. To combat this problem, some cast iron pots and pans come lined with enamel. The enamel, however, can chip.

Glass. Glass is a hard, smooth surface that does not react chemically with either food acids or alkalis. Although glass can transmit heat quickly and directly, it is a poor choice because it does not transfer heat throughout the pot or pan well. The one cooktop exception is the glass double boiler. It allows the cook to closely monitor the rate at which the water is boiling below, while watching how the food in the upper chamber is doing. Although heat is absorbed only through the glass bottom and diffusion is poor, in a double boiler this problem is relatively minor. You can accomplish careful and controlled cooking in a glass double boiler, and that is all that matters.

One caution about glass: When you heat a glass pot or pan on the cooktop or in the oven, always add liquid to it. Without any liquid, glass will become overheated and weaken, and likely crack or break on next use. If you forget to add liquid or the liquid has evaporated, you should throw the pot or pan away.

Aluminum. Aluminum is an excellent heat conductor and diffuser. The metal is lightweight, yet tough, and can be used effectively for sauces, omelettes, stews, casseroles and sauté work. However, aluminum's major drawback is that it reacts chemically with acids and can darken, discolor and change the taste of some acidic foods. A white sauce, for example, may turn gray in an aluminum pot if you've made a tomato sauce in it a week or two earlier. For that reason, some people keep their aluminum pots and pans separated for different uses.

An acceptable alternative is aluminum lined with stainless steel. With those pots and pans, you have aluminum's superlative heat distribution property combined with stainless steel's non-absorbency. If you are interested in that combination, make sure the aluminum covers the stainless steel fully because stainless steel pans made with aluminum only on the bottom do not effectively conduct heat up the sides. One of the best lines on the market is a three ply bonded design that sandwiches a pure aluminum core between exterior and interior layers of stainless steel. Those pots and pans work on any cooktop, including magnetic induction. Most important, even a burnt pan will clean easily and beautifully. They are pricey, but worth it.

Copper. Copper is a wonderful metal for cooktop use. It absorbs heat quickly, diffuses it evenly, and dissipates it rapidly. But copper must be lined because it chemically reacts with certain foods and can create toxins. You will generally find copper pots and pans lined with tin, stainless steel or even silver. The quality of the copper can be measured by its feel–*i.e.*, the heavier the copper the better.

Copper is also a beautiful sight to present to guests. However, it is very expensive and requires constant maintenance. Its surface must be cleaned with a copper cleaner, or salt and vinegar, or lemon juice to keep it shiny. A silver or tin lining must be watched because it will wear out and the pot or pan will need to be resilvered or retinned, which is also costly. Sometimes you will find a copper pot lined with aluminum. The combination is wasted, since copper and aluminum both conduct heat well, and aluminum has that absorbency problem. Also stay away from stainless steel pans that feature a coating of copper on the bottom. You'll pay for the copper, which is too thin to do any good, and you're stuck with stainless steel's drawbacks.

I personally prefer a high quality copper pan with a stainless steel lining because it should never need replacing. Copper pots never need high heat; medium heat is more than adequate.

Non-stick. Although non-stick pans are very popular especially for people who are on a diet, I don't particularly like them. They change the texture of some foods and, in my book, their ease of cleaning is simply not a good enough trade-off. There are any number of non-stick vegetable sprays on the market today, and they even come with garlic butter flavoring and olive oil. If you are diligent about using them, you will never have a clean-up problem. A good quality pot or pan requires virtually no more maintenance than a non-stick one and will stand up to much greater abuse.

Pots and pans are complex equipment because you have to think carefully about what you want to cook and how you will cook it. I've summed it up for you in Chart 1. (See page 67.)

Knives

You cannot cook well without good knives. Period. Notice that I use the plural. There's nothing wrong with having one good, all-purpose knife that you feel comfortable using. However, one knife will not address all your cooking needs. Specific knives are designed for specific tasks. Take advantage of the many options you can find at a good kitchen or specialty store.

When shopping for knives, you want to buy a forged, rather than a stamped knife. Forged knives are made from one piece of metal, whereas a stamped knife may be made from several pieces and so is more likely to break. The solid piece construction of a forged knife makes it stronger. It has superior weight and balance, which translates into less stress on your hand.

A sure sign of a quality knife is the collar, or the edge of the knife, that butts up against your hand on the underside. A good knife will feature a one-half inch thick collar, large enough to fit the hand comfortably. The blade should extend into a triple riveted wood–not plastic–handle which yields better traction for greasy hands. A quality knife will feel balanced, neither heavier at the tip nor at the handle.

Most knives today are made from a combination of carbon and stainless steel. A full carbon knife will rust if not immediately cleaned and dried after use. A combination with stainless steel alleviates that problem.

The key to a good knife is sharpness. Whenever you use one, you need to straighten or steel the blade edge, called the feather. This is done with an instrument called a steel, or round, which is an elongated steel rod with a rough grained surface designed to maintain a blade's sharpness. To straighten the feather, you lay the knife on the rod and stroke at an angle with an upward and downward motion. If you are diligent about doing this, your knives will stay sharper longer.

To maintain their effectiveness, knives need to be stored properly. The best all-around knife storage system is a magnetic bar that is designed to maintain the feather. Magnetic bars can be affixed to cabinet sides, to a wall or in a drawer. Placing two bars roughly seven inches apart will enable you to attach an eight inch or longer knife, such as a chef's knife, bread knife or slicer. The top bar holds the blade, the bottom holds the handle. Smaller

(continue on page 68)

Pots and Pans

Material	Heat Dispersion/ Dissipation	Where To Use	Comments	Suggested Use
Stainless Steel	Poor	Stovetop; oven	Needs to be combined with a metal alloy, such as aluminum or copper	Water for pasta, soups
Cast iron	Excellent dispersion; poor dissipation	Stovetop; oven	Not good for sautéing, excellent for oven use, requires careful use if lined with enamel, which can chip	Pan frying, braising, stews, pancakes
Glass	Poor	Stovetop	Best use is as a double boiler	Casseroles, microwave
Aluminum	Excellent	Stovetop; oven, if lined with stainless steel	Leaches acidic foods if not lined with stainless steel	Boiling, poaching, sautéing, steaming, dark sauces, light sauces if lined with stainless steel
Copper	Excellent	Stovetop; oven	Toxic with most food unless lined with tin, silver, or stainless steel, avoid high heat, tarnishes	Boiling, poaching, sautéing, steaming, sauces
Non-stick	Good	Stovetop	Not good for high heat use since fluorocarbon materials will decompose and emit noxious vapors above 500 degrees F., can change the texture of some foods	Sautéing without fats

CHART 1

knives will fit completely on one of the bars.

Often, people store their knives in wood knife blocks that sit on the countertop. The advantage is the easy accessibility of the knives. However, every time you pull out a knife from one of those blocks, the edge scrapes the slot's interior and distorts the feather. To avoid that, simply store your knives with the blade up.

Another type of knife storage unit consists of a simple slotted bar with a protective front shield that hangs on a wall or the side of a cabinet. Those bars are manufactured in solid surface materials–wood and stainless steel to match different kitchen decors. But, as with wood blocks, any time a knife is pulled from its slot, it should be steeled.

You can also find, in restaurant supply houses and some gourmet kitchen shops, fabric knife cases with plastic lined pockets. Those cases roll up for easy storage. The negative is that it's difficult getting to a single knife.

Finally, many people, unfortunately, simply toss their knives into a drawer without thought. There is some hope for all of you. A few cabinet companies now make a wooden board, slotted along the top, that fits into a kitchen drawer. Knives can be slipped into the drawer horizontally, so their blades are held firmly in the slots. But again, those knives should be steeled before use. Of course, little of this advice applies to poor quality knives. You simply can't improve their performance. A good knife, on the other hand, with proper care, will last a lifetime. I am still using the very first knife I bought for the cooking school I attended 45 years ago.

Knives, like pots and pans, are the most basic, yet overlooked, tools in the kitchen. In Chart 2, page 69, I give you the basic set I recommend.

Knives

Type	Blade Size	Total Size	Use
French	6 to 8 inches, whichever is most comfortable in your hand	13 to 19 inches	Slicing, dicing, chopping
Paring	2-1/2 to 4 inches	6 to 10 inches	Slicing, dicing small items
Slicer	8 to 10 inches	15 to 17 inches	Cooked meats
Serrated	8 inches	12 to 13 inches	Bread, tomatoes
Steel	10 to 14 inches	20 inches	Straightening the feather of a blade

CHART 2

Notes

WORKING WITH A DESIGNER

Finding the right kitchen designer is not simply a matter of finding someone who understands budgets and materials. Sad to say, few in the kitchen design industry ever even talk about the cooking process. Most kitchen designers understand the kitchen from the technical side only. In other words, they may understand all the parts without understanding the whole. However, a kitchen is more than the sum of its parts.

If cooking is a priority to you, the key to finding the right kitchen designer is asking the right questions: "Do you cook?" Or, if you are asking for a referral, "Do you know of a kitchen designer who understands the complexity of cooking and baking?"

In other words, can this designer efficiently create, shop for, cook and clean up a somewhat complex meal for eight or more? You want someone who will consider such issues as where the microwave is in relation to the refrigerator and whether you can sauté and bake at the same time. You want someone who understands what poaching and grilling mean and what making a soufflé is all about.

I'd be kidding if I said it would be easy to find such a person. Your best sources are through personal referrals, cooking schools, and the National Kitchen and Bath Association (NKBA). The NKBA, which encompasses a whole range of professionals and companies that manufacture kitchen products, plays a large role in the education of the kitchen designer, including the certification, CKD (Certified Kitchen Designer), that you see after my name on the cover of this book.

To attain the CKD designation of excellence and achievement, a designer must fulfill the following requirements:

- Seven years of experience or education in the kitchen industry, with at least two years of experience in design, planning and installation supervision of residential kitchens;
- Two complete sets of approved drawing documents from actual designed, planned and installed residential kitchen projects;
- Two consumer references pertaining to projects the designer has completed for a consumer;
- Two professional affidavits submitted by allied professionals regarding the designer's competency and work ethics;
- Passage of a day long, comprehensive examination on the specialized discipline of residential kitchen design, planning and installation supervision; and
- Adherence to the NKBA's code of professional conduct.

Being a member of the NKBA, I am certain it can take the one criticism I have of the organization: Its curriculum does not include instruction in the processes of cooking or baking. These things must be taught for a kitchen designer to be truly knowledgeable. I am hopeful that classes in these disciplines will soon become mandatory for a CKD designation.

Because of the excellent job the NKBA does perform educating kitchen designers in the construction, technical, and cabinetry arenas of the kitchen world, I would only recommend that you interview at least two or three CKDs. When you find someone you feel comfortable with, ask for the names of three clients who have had jobs completed within the past year. Call those clients to see if they'll let you drop by to see the work.

Then ask them key questions: Did the designer understand the cooking process? Was he or she knowledgeable about appliances? Did the designer stay within budget? Was the design completed within the specified time? Was the designer patient, punctual and in all ways professional? Did you get what you wanted?

When you've chosen your designer, prioritize where you want your dollars to go–*i.e.*, space flow, appliances, cabinetry, countertops and flooring. A good designer will be realistic with your budget. If, for example, your budget is $30,000 and the items you've chosen add up to $60,000, a knowledgeable designer should be able to offer you some options. Keep in mind, however, that you will never be able to get a $60,000 job for $30,000. If any designer promises that, run for your life.

The Full Service Designer

Before you set out to hire a kitchen designer, you need to decide what it is you want done. If, for example, you simply want a facelift with new paint, countertops, flooring and window treatment, then you don't need a designer. An interior decorator (who doesnt make structural changes) will do. If, however, you intend to move or replace appliances, reconfigure your kitchen layout or knock through walls, you should consult a kitchen designer. If the work involves knowledge of basic house construction, the kitchen designer may also need to work with an architect or engineer.

The type of designer I am, and the type I am recommending you try to find, is what I like to call a full service designer. I am unusual in that I am a chef and care passionately about cooking. My professional obsession is that my clients should be able to use and enjoy their kitchens as much as, or even more than I do my own. It will come as no surprise, then, that I believe a good kitchen designer should cook with each and every client before putting pencil to paper. I invite my clients into my own kitchen, so they can experience what I consider good space layout and appliances. In turn, I am educated by my clients on the subject of their needs and goals for their new kitchens.

After the first session in my kitchen, I present clients with a questionnaire. It is not only a terrific way for clients to communicate to me what they feel they need, but the questions help us both discover what they want. After going over the questionnaire, I then measure the job site. I take photographs to use as references that remind me of what goes on beyond the kitchen–in the dining room, in the living room and outside the windows and doors.

The next step is typically to go appliance shopping. By now you know that I believe appliances should drive the design. I simply cannot understand what to do with a kitchen space until I know which appliances are going into that space. I have found that a good looking design that simply leaves holes for the appliances may look spectacular but probably won't cook well.

With the appliance information in hand, I am then able to do rough plans, which enables the client to see on paper where everything goes. This I call our "conversation plan." I explain what I've done and why. The client can then say, "I like it," "I don't like it," or, in most cases, "I like this but can we move that?" The basic floor plan is worked out to both our satisfaction and, at that point, we go cabinet shopping.

Now we are looking at pure style, and the client is fully in charge. All I'm looking for is what type of door style the client chooses, whether the cabinets are framed or frameless, and whether the chosen cabinet line poses any design limitations for such elements as angles or curved radii.

Once the cabinets are chosen, I draw up a proper floor plan and open elevations. This is a straight-on view of the cabinets without doors drawn, in order to show the shelving configurations inside the cabinets. These open elevations present a second conversation opportunity. The client and I discuss what goes into each and every cabinet–*i.e.*, drawers, rollout shelves, silverware holder, location of trays and so on. Once this task is accomplished, we go shopping for the right countertop surface, for flooring and for window treatments.

I am now ready to assemble a complete set of plans, which will include a floor plan and elevations created to the specifications of the cabinets that the client has chosen. The plans also include perspective drawings so that the client can clearly see how the kitchen will look, plus mechanical, electrical, lighting, and finally, demolition plans. (See the complete set of plans at the end of this chapter, starting on page 75.)

With the kitchen plans package complete, it is time to bring in contractor bids. This job generally falls to the client, although I will in all cases help interview if it is desired. Once the client has chosen the contractor, the project is underway. I remain available throughout the construction phase should a problem or other need arise.

When the kitchen is finished, I usually take my client shopping for pots, pans, knives and any other appliances they may lack or need to replace. The final service I provide is to cook a meal for 8 to 12 guests with the client. That gives me the chance to help them adapt to the new kitchen, teach them about their new appliances and perhaps even give them a more efficient way to cook.

There, in a nutshell, is my process. On average, it requires 75 to 100 hours for the simpler jobs and, for more complex projects, between 175 and 250 hours. Every designer works differently. The key is that you convey your needs and wishes. Do not feel shy about being assertive, offering suggestions and insisting on joint decision making. Educating yourself is the only way you can become partners with your kitchen designer and end up with a *Kitchen Design with Cooking in Mind*.

How a Design Fee Is Calculated

Designers offer their time, knowledge, creativity, experience and sources. I divide my sources into two catagories: High blood pressure and low blood pressure. Guess who I go to.

If a designer's profit comes from selling you certain products, it will undoubtedly limit creativity. That is why I have chosen to work the way I do and why I recommend you work with a designer at an agreed upon hourly rate or a flat rate for the whole job. A significant amount of time goes into accomplishing a good kitchen design. The following is a breakdown of my process:

1. Consultation–Determining what the client wants, needs and how much they can spend: 5-15 hours
2. Cooking with the client in my kitchen–Talking with the client about kitchen design in the context of cooking: 4-6 hours
3. Shopping for appliances–Making the client aware of what's available in the marketplace: 4-6 hours
4. Creating and presenting the rough flow plan–Showing the client where the appliances go and what the traffic patterns will be: 15-50 hours
5. Shopping for cabinetry–Taking the client to various showrooms that carry cabinetry within the budget: 5-15 hours
6. Layout, open elevations and perspectives–Illustrating for the client on paper just how the kitchen will look: 10-20 hours
7. Plan review–Planning with the client what goes into every drawer and cabinet and what special cabinetry is needed: 2-6 hours
8. Shopping for countertops and flooring: 5-15 hours
9. Reviewing lighting, electrical and mechanical plans: 5-10 hours
10. Interviewing contractors: 2-6 hours
11. Following through on job completion: 20-60 hours
12. Shopping for small wares: 3-5 hours
13. Cooking dinner in the client's new kitchen: 6-8 hours

KITCHEN AS IS PLUS CONSTRUCTION DOCUMENT

151 3/4"
95 1/4"
28"
20 1/2"
2 7/6"
30"
73"
203/16"
30"
27 5/16"
30"
10 5/16"
22 1/4"
56"
20 3/4"
99"

EXISTING DOOR
NEW 2 LITE FR. DOORS
CLOSE WINDOW
REMOVE
REMOVE
CLOSE DOOR
131/16"
EXISTING DOOR
CEILING HT. 79"
EXISTING WINDOWS 2
SILLS OA 36"
30"
36 1/4"
94 1/6"
57"
NEW DOOR
NEW CLOSET SHELVING AND POLE
10 1/2"
32"
15 1/4"
CLOSE DOOR
59"
REMOVE WALL & HEADER OVER DOOR IF A BEAM IS REQUIRED, THEN CONSTR. W CLG.
EXISTING WINDOWS
30"
10"
EXISTING DOORS
55 1/2"
30"
77"
162 1/2"

FOR THE RESIDENCE OF   DON AND SALLY SILVERS
AT

APPROVED BY   DATE

D.E. SILVERS

155 SOUTH ORANGE DRIVE
LOS ANGELES, CA 90036

PH# 323.934.4761
FAX# 323.934.0215

NEW KITCHEN

CONTINUOUS SHELF AROUND KITCHEN PERIMETER

CUSTOM WOOD HOOD
STAINLESS STEEL LINER AND BLOWER

CHAR BROILER

COOKTOP OVEN

POT FILLER

PREP SINK

DW

CLEAN-UP SINK
SECONDARY PREP SINK

COUNTER HEIGHT 34"

OVEN
UNDER COUNTER

MICRO

REF

JOB SITE ADDRESS

TEL ( )

HOME
OFFICE

DRAWN BY: JOHN

DATE: 12/17/93

SCALE: 1/2"=1'-0"

REVISED: 1 2 3 4 5 6

THIS DRAWING IS THE EXCLUSIVE PROPERTY OF D.E. SILVERS

SHEET NO. OF

CERTIFIED
DONALD E. SILVERS
REGISTER NO.
KITCHEN DESIGNER

FOR THE RESIDENCE OF   DON AND SALLY SILVERS
AT

APPROVED BY   DATE

D.E. SILVERS
155 SOUTH ORANGE DRIVE
LOS ANGELES, CA 90036
PH# 323.934.4761
FAX# 323.934.0215

PERSPECTIVE 1

JOB SITE ADDRESS

TEL
( )
( )

HOME
OFFICE

DRAWN BY:
JOHN

DATE:
12/17/93

SCALE:
1/2"=1'-0"

REVISED:
1 2 3
4 5 6

SHEET
NO.
OF

FOR THE RESIDENCE OF   DON AND SALLY SILVERS
AT

APPROVED BY   DATE

D.E. SILVERS

155 SOUTH ORANGE DRIVE   PH# 323.934.4761
LOS ANGELES, CA 90036   FAX# 323.934.0215

PERSPECTIVE 2

FOR THE RESIDENCE OF   DON AND SALLY SILVERS
AT

APPROVED BY   DATE

D.E. SILVERS

155 SOUTH ORANGE DRIVE
LOS ANGELES, CA 90036

PH# 323.934.4761
FAX# 323.934.0215

CERTIFIED
DONALD E. SILVERS, INC.
REGISTR. NO. 100879
KITCHEN DESIGNER

OPEN ELEVATIONS

FOR THE RESIDENCE OF **DON AND SALLY SILVERS**
AT

APPROVED BY   DATE

D.E. SILVERS

155 SOUTH ORANGE DRIVE
LOS ANGELES, CA 90036

PH# 323.934.4761
FAX# 323.934.0215

80

LIGHTING PLAN

NOTE: ALL UNDER CABINET LIGHTS TO BE STUBBED OUT @ 53½" AFF USING ⅜Ø FLEX.

LIGHTING IN HOOD AREA BY HOOD FABRICATOR.

HANGING FIXTURE

JOB SITE ADDRESS					
TEL ( ) ( )	HOME OFFICE	DRAWN BY: JOHN	DATE: 12/17/93	SCALE: 1/2"=1'-0"	REVISED:

1	2	3
4	5	6

SHEET NO. OF

FOR THE RESIDENCE OF DON AND SALLY SILVERS
AT
APPROVED BY DATE

D.E. SILVERS

155 SOUTH ORANGE DRIVE
LOS ANGELES, CA 90036

PH# 323.934.4761
FAX# 323.934.0215

CERTIFIED KITCHEN DESIGNER

ELECTRICAL AND MECHANICAL PLAN

YOUR KITCHEN QUESTIONNAIRE

The following survey should help you determine your needs and answer questions about any kitchen designer you are considering working with. In fact, if the kitchen designer doesn't ask or care about these issues, keep looking!

1. How many eat at home on a daily basis?
Monday___Tuesday___Wednesday___Thursday___Friday_____Saturday___Sunday_____
Breakfast_____ Lunch_____ Dinner_____

2. How often, and for how many, do you entertain informally?
Weekly_____Bi-monthly_____ Monthly_____
1-3_____ 4-6_____ 7 or more_____

3. What is a sample informal dinner menu?
_____
_____

4. What is a favorite entree you serve for an informal dinner?
_____
_____

5. How often, and for how many, do you entertain formally?
Weekly_____Bi-monthly_____Monthly_____
1-3_____ 4-6_____ 7 or more_____

6. When you cook formally, how many people help in the kitchen? _____

7. What is a sample formal dinner menu?
_____
_____

8. What is a favorite entree you serve for a formal dinner?
_____
_____

9. What is a sample menu you would prepare for the family?

_____

_____

10. Would you create any different menus with a new kitchen? _____

11. What appliance do you like to work with most? _____

12. What appliance do you like to work with least? _____

13. What appliance that you don't have would you most like to have? _____

14. Do you prefer to sit or stand while doing prep work? _____

15. Are you right or left handed? _____

16. Who in the family is the primary cook? _____

17. How tall is the primary cook? _____

18. Does the primary cook have any physical limitations? Please tell me in detail.

_____

19. What don't you like about your present kitchen?

_____

_____

20. What do you like most about your present kitchen?

_____

_____

21. What are the reasons you would want to change your kitchen?

_____

_____

22. Do you like to work in your kitchen alone or to have guests visiting with you or helping you while you cook? _____

23. What kind of access would you like your kitchen to have to adjacent rooms?

_____

_____

24. What type of feeling would you like your new kitchen to have? Please circle.

Contemporary   Family Retreat

Open and Airy   Traditional

Warm and Cozy Country   Formal

Personal Design Statement   Other _____

25. What colors do you like?_____

   Dislike?_____

26. Do you want to relocate or change doors, windows, or walls?

_____

_____

27. Do you need an area in your kitchen to plan menus, store cookbooks or serve any other purpose?_____

28. How often do you grocery shop?

Daily_____Bi-weekly_____Weekly_____

29. What percentages of frozen, canned, and fresh foods do you buy?

Frozen_____ Canned_____ Fresh_____

30. Do you have enough storage space? _____

31. How many sets of dishes or china do you have?_____

32. How many sets of glassware or crystal do you have?_____

33. How many sets of flatware or silverware do you have?_____

34. Do you have any other storage space for these items than in the kitchen?_____

35. Do you do any of the following?

Can____ Make candy____ Bake____ Make pasta____

Dehydrate food____ Make ice cream____ Make stock____ Other_____

36. Do you, or do you want to, recycle any of the following?

Plastic____ Clear glass____ Green glass____ Brown glass____

Paper____ Compact refuse____ Other _____

37. Do you have, or would you like, a sorting station in any of these areas?

Kitchen____ Garage____ Utility room____ Basement____ Other _____

38. Do you have any of the following small wares? Do you store them on the counter or in a cabinet?

Blender _____

Bread machine _____

Can opener _____

Coffee grinder _____

Crepe maker _____

Crockpot _____

Deep-fat fryer _____

Dehydrator _____

Electric frying pan _____

Espresso machine _____

Food grinder _____

Food processor _____

Food slicer _____

Griddle _____

Hand mixer _____

Ice cream maker _____

Ice crusher _____

Immersion blender _____

Juicer _____

Knife sharpener _____

Pasta machine _____

Pizza stone _____

Popcorn maker _____

Sandwich maker _____

Scale _____

Steamer _____

Toaster _____

Toaster oven _____

Waffle maker _____

Wok _____

Yogurt maker _____

Other _____

39. Which, if any, of the following would you like in your kitchen?

Study area_____ Sewing area_____ Laundry area_____ Ironing board_____ Stereo_____

Computer_____ Television_____ Plants/herbs_____ Telephone_____ Other _____

40. List every item in your kitchen, indicating its frequency of use and where it is stored.

Used daily=D   Used within the week=W   Used within the month=M   Used occasionally=O

Wall cabinet=WC   Laundry=L   Basement=B   Appliance garage=AG

Countertop=CT   Base cabinet=BC   Desk=DK   Tall cabinet=TC

Everyday Dishes _____

_____

_____

China _____

_____

Everyday glasses _____

_____

Crystal _____

_____

Flatware _____

_____

Silverware _____

_____

Pots _____

_____

Pans _____

_____

Trays _____

_____

Serving pieces _____

_____

Storage containers _____

_____

Knives _____

_____

_____

Utensils _____

_____

_____

Baking pans _____

_____

_____

Other _____

_____

_____

41. Where do you currently store the following?

Boxed goods _____

Canned goods _____

Cleaning supplies _____

Linens _____

Laundry soaps _____

Non-refrigerated fruits and vegetables _____

Paper products _____

Pet food _____

Recyclable containers _____

Spices _____

Table appointments _____

Wrapping materials _____

Other _____

NAME _____

ADDRESS _____

CITY & STATE _____

HOME PHONE _____

BUSINESS PHONE _____

CELL PHONE _____

FAX _____

E-MAIL _____

BOOKS AVAILABLE FROM NMI PUBLISHERS

BUYING RETAIL IS STUPID!
Where to Buy Everything at Giant Savings in Southern California
by Trisha King-Crumley, Deborah Newmark, and Bonnie Cunningham
(498 pages, Third Edition ... $16.95)

This best selling regional book includes over 2,100 stores and outlets where you can buy EVERYTHING from A to Z antiques, appliances, building materials, electronics, furniture, groceries, jewelry, luggage, musical instruments, pets, sporting goods, wallpaper, and much more at savings from 20% to 80% off retail prices. Also includes 150 mail order discount businesses from which you can buy all the above at great savings.

HAPPINESS THROUGH SUPERFICIALITY
The War Against Meaningful Relationships
by Jerry Newmark and Irving S. Newmark
(176 pages, 1992 ... $11.95)

This book lifts your spirits, makes you laugh, challenges you to rethink your values, and shows you how to lead a happier, more fulfilling life. The Doctors Newmark offer fresh perspectives, in numerous and often provocative ways, on many of the most serious aspects of life sex, marriage, parenting, work, health, education, money, love, lawyers, doctors, psychotherapy, and much more. You will learn how to stop taking everything too seriously, especially yourself and how to become through the 1990s whole and happy.

THIS SCHOOL BELONGS TO YOU & ME:
Every Learner A Teacher, Every Teacher A Learner
by Gerald Newmark
(431 pages, 1976 ... $9.95)

First published in 1976, this book remains an important resource for anyone interested in improving education. It describes a new kind of learning community, an exciting school where students, parents, teachers, staff, and administrators are turned on to learning and to working cooperatively with each other.

"This School Belongs To You & Me" offers a detailed plan for the redesign of an entire school into a vibrant learning community. It is also a rich resource book of educational ideas and practices which can be used by individual teachers to improve an existing program or classroom. Developed from a seven year Ford Foundation supported project in inner-city elementary schools, the ideas presented can be applied to all school levels–whatever their geographic, ethnic, or soci-economic characteristics–in exciting, cost-effective ways.

To order any of the above books, send a check for the amount indicated, plus $3.00 for postage & handling (add $1 for each additional book) to NMI PUBLISHERS, 18345 Ventura Blvd., Suite 314, Tarzana, CA 91356. For credit card orders, call 818-708-1244.

If you would like additional copies of *Kitchen Design with Cooking in Mind* or are interested in the Consultation and Design Services of Donald E. Silvers, CKD, call 800-900-4761.

Write to Donald E. Silvers, **KITCHEN DESIGN WITH COOKING IN MIND**, 155 S. Orange Dr., Los Angeles, CA 90036.

March 2, 1995

Mr. Don E. Silvers
155 South Orange Drive
Los Angeles, CA 90036

Dear Don,

You truly have been a life saver to me. I bought a home that had a kitchen designed by one of the better known kitchen designers in my city that made cooking a true chore. Thus, I decided to redo my kitchen. But, after going through two successive architects, I still didn't have a design that felt right. One Sunday, I came upon an article in our paper that simply said if you want to design your kitchen right you need the book on kitchen designs by Don Silvers. At that point, I was game for anything.

I sent for your book and found it extremely enlightening. Due to my hectic schedule and my loss of faith in the ability of architects designing kitchens, I asked and was pleasantly surprised, when you agreed to help me in my design. I truly feel comfortable with what you have done and can imagine stress free cooking in your wonderfully laid out kitchen that incorporated all of my needs and made the kitchen finally workable. I can't wait until the project is done.

I do want to thank you for all of your continual follow up and genuine interest in making sure this project comes out correctly. You sure have proven the axiom "don't believe everything you read in the paper" to be false.

Sincerely,
EAGLE CRUSHER COMPANY, INC.

Susanne Cobey
President/CEO

SC:rjg

4250 S.R. 309 • GALION, OHIO 44B33 • FAX (419) 4BB-4B40 • (419) 4BB-22BB

specializing in Self-Contained, Portable Crushing & Screening Plants for Recycle (Concrete, Asphalt. Rubble) and Hard Rock Crushing (Open Pit & Veep Mine)
Custom-Engineered Stationary and Portable Crushing Systems - Equipment & Parts (Eagle, Austin-Western, Diamond, Madsen, & Scoopmobile)

Pamela A. Bruning, CLU, ChFC
Managing Director

Buckeye Agency
Suite 170, 2600 Corporate Exchange Drive
Columbus, OH 43231~1670
Office: 614-895-3830 Ext. 1202
Fax: 614-895-3823

February 28, 1995

Donald Silvers, CKD
155 South Orange Drive
Los Angeles, CA 90036

Dear Don:

It is with a great deal of pleasure that I wish to take a few moments to thank you for your invaluable contributions to the "heart" of our new home - the kitchen.

It was pure chance that led me to read the newspaper that one Sunday (a luxury I usually don't have) and the article in it about you. After sending off for your book, reading it, and being very impressed with your ideas on REAL kitchens for people who REALLY cook, I decided to pursue utilization of your special talents.

I have been totally delighted with your ideas, your creativity, your responsiveness and your general professionalism. I have retained the series of drawings of our kitchen floor plan as they progressed from the initial architects rendering I sent to you to the final plan that is currently being built. It is amazing how much more functional and even more beautiful the space has become since you've been working on it. I was so frustrated initially with the plans submitted by our architect's and builder; here we were going to put all of this money into a house and I had a kitchen that did not "feel" right - and didn't know what to do about it!

Now I'm looking at the plans of the space I cannot wait to get into. The suggestions on design, on features, on layout and on over all work patterns of the space have been invaluable. The mare fact that you saved us from spending thousands of dollars on the wrong model commercial stove has repaid my initial investment in you many times over. Your suggestions on sources for cabinetry and interior options have resulted in a kitchen that will truly be a joy to work in.

Don, I don't know how many people in this country do what you do. I could wish there would be many, many more - as there would be many more families who would be as thrilled with their new homes as we will be. Until that happens, I can only hope that others like me, couples like Mac and I who are serious about our kitchens, have the good fortune to run into you. I wish you all the best in the future - may your business grow and prosper. If I ever build another home, rest assured that I will locate you, wherever you are, before I even begin to think about a builder.

Sincerely,

Pamela A. Bruning, CLU, ChFC

THE SEALE ORGANIZATION

280 Camino Sur
Palm Springs, CA 92262
(760) 325-3519
Fax (760) 320-0610

March 12,1998

Donald E. Silvers, CKD
155 South Orange Drive
Los Angeles, CA 90036

Dear Don:

Our new functional kitchen you designed is finished. It is incredibly beautiful proving that you can have the best of both worlds. Thank you for designing it and walking me through all the steps. With your expertise, we achieved a result even better than anticipated within budget without compromising on anything.

Having been in the design and remodeling business, I have renovated many kitchens, replacing what the builder did. When it came to designing my own kitchen from scratch, I did not know where to begin. Fortunately I read your book ***Kitchen Design With Cooking In Mind***. While I learned a lot from your book, I realized with the money I intended to spend, I wanted you to design it. Without your expertise, costly mistakes, far in excess of your fees, would have been made.

With your expertise, design, and contacts, we were able to produce a "world class" kitchen more economically than would have been possible had I tried to "wing it alone." Many people take the "do it yourself" approach with a new kitchen because they think a certified kitchen designer is expensive. Not so! He who designs it himself, in my opinion, is a fool - even if he has design experience! Kitchen design is a specialty.

What sets you apart from other kitchen designers is your seasoned experience as a professional chef. Everything you put in the plan was logical and had a purpose for being there. Your advice on cabinet and appliance selection is invaluable.

Enclosed are some print outs of digital photographs. After decorative accessories are in, it will be professionally photographed, should you wish to use it in your new book.

Many thank to you, my friend, for a project well done!

Sincerely,

Robert M. Seale

Jose & Pamela David
7339 West Green Lake Drive North
Seattle, Washington 98103

March 1, 2001

Donald E. Silvers
155 South Orange Drive
Los Angeles, CA 90036

Dear Don,

We have been in our newly remodeled kitchen now for two years. For those two years as I work in my lovely and very efficient kitchen I think to myself that I need to write Don to tell him how pleased I am with how my kitchen works.
Today is the day.

Your advice from choosing appliances to cabinet layout was very helpful. I especially enjoy the pull out pantry, since I couldn't have cabinets above my prep area that 12" of storage really packs it in and makes for less travel to find needed ingredients. The best part of the entire kitchen is the two sinks located in each corner of the kitchen. The prep area is separated from the clean-up area and each functions very well. My very compact primary prep area is SO efficient. I don't have to take but 1/2 step to the refrigerator, sink and range yet as you said four or five people can work in the kitchen. The layout works beautifully for our gourmet group's dinners as well as our daily family meals (with help from my two young boys).

Hiring you to plan the kitchen was the best spent dollars of the entire remodel!

Sincerely,
Pamela David

Our family decided to make the move from Los Angeles, California to Nashville, Tennessee. We anticipated many changes. Topping our list was finding a place to live. We agreed on the location. Now we needed to find a house that would accommodate our lifestyle; a house with a kitchen and floor plan that allowed us to host gatherings of all sizes.

We looked at dozens of homes ranging from 1800's historical homes to newly built custom homes, all boasting of renovated or existing gourmet kitchens. We soon found this to mean a beautifully appointed space equipped with the latest appliances needed to reheat already prepared foods.

By prioritizing the importance of aesthetics over thoughtful planning and quality products, this type of kitchen limited my options as a cook.

The decision was made that we would settle into a temporary living situation while developing plans to build our own home. I began collecting pictures and articles with ideas we could incorporate into our house plans. In the process, I read several kitchen design books. The one that proved most helpful to me was <u>Kitchen Design with Cooking in Mind</u> by Don Silvers. The information Don laid out in his book gave me the foundation I needed to create a family cooking environment that would prove to be the heart of our home for many years to come.

I compiled my wish list. I wanted a kitchen that was:

1. user friendly
2. to provide an intimate family atmosphere, yet would accommodate parties of 8 to 80 without overload.
3. I wanted appliances that could stand the test of time while providing me with an attractive environment in which to work.
4. I wanted efficient and well-organized work and storage space, making clean-up easy for anyone using the kitchen.
5. I wanted a floor plan that tastefully united the kitchen and adjoining rooms in the house.
6. Finally, I wanted a cooking environment that gives guests the opportunity to help cook or simply sit nearby and visit, allowing me to enjoy their company without having to maneuver around them while preparing the meal.

Now all I needed to do was to get my totally overwhelming kitchen concept together and hand it over to Don. We planned a trip back to L.A. Don's passion for educating people to fine foods along with his gift of creating a personalized environment that enhances the abilities of any cook quickly became evident. The concerns we had of Don being in another state during the building process were put to rest as soon as we saw Don's plans. Our architect noted the attention Don paid in providing such detailed blueprints. If a question arose on the job site, we called Don and he addressed the situation with concise clarity, getting everything back on track. With the aid of phone, faxes and Fed Ex our project with Don was free of glitches. I only wish the rest of the house came together so effortlessly.

I have numerous examples of brining in ideas I had pulled together for my kitchen, and Don understanding what I was trying to accomplish. He demonstrated how, in certain situations, I was actually working against myself. The best example of this is in regard to my plan was in dealing with my pantry. I had designed an 8' by 9' walk-in pantry, which I was thrilled about. It would hold everything: canned goods, paper goods, dog food, overnight guests....The possibilities were endless!

After reviewing my blueprints Don suggested that I relocate my pantry to a built-in roll-out cabinet space, enclosing a hutch I could display dishes in. This would free up the 8' by 9' space to be a baking room. I paused, caught my breath, and reasoned....yes, I love to bake. In fact, I'm a serious baker. But give up my pantry? That was a hard one for me. Don assured me that I'd have more than enough storage space. As a result of Don's engineering, my pantry is the highlight of kitchen. I'm thrilled with my baking room, and our overnight guests enjoy a spacious guest room upstairs.

We moved in over a year ago and, without hesitation my family would say that the kitchen is the most lived-in space of our home. Whether it's homework, after-school snacks, late-night talks or dinner parties, our kitchen is truly the heart of our home.

We are grateful to Don for Giving us an environment where our family and friends can gather, creating memories we will cherish throughout our lives. Don, our sincere thanks.

Dori Howard
Brentwood, Tennessee

9 Turret Lane
Woodbury, New York 11797

Donal Silvers,CKD
155 South Orange Drive
Los Angeles, CA 90036

Dear Don:

The cabinets which you helped me research are finally on order as are my appliances. I'm in a holding pattern now waiting for everything to come in and for my contractor to give me the definitive start date. With time on my hands I felt the need to take time to reflect on the help and support that you have given me.

I fear that without your input from the beginning I would have spent a lot more money on everything as I felt that I hate to use a full service design center. As you guided me, it became clear that I was giving someone more money than necessary for cabinets that I was able to obtain for less and for design advice from someone who had never cooked in his own kitchen. I needed some courage to walk away from that situation but, because of your guidance and availability of your time for in-depth conversations, I am pulling this whole thing together myself armed with a fresh viewpoint and confidence.

The time I spent with you in California was invaluable but what is most impressive to me is that you have been available since to answer some of my questions both new and old and to provide me with sources to further research areas of concern. Every person that you have put me in touch with has been professional and courteous and willing to provide information whether or not a purchase was made. The thing that has held me back the most has been my own difficulty making decisions but you have even helped me further by offering pros and cons of each side of the decision. You have helped me save money in area where there would be little "bang for the buck," and explained where the dollars would be well spent. It has been amazing to me that on every detail you have clear and concise reasons why you do what you do. It appears that everything in the kitchens you plan has a reason and you have made those reasons very clear to understand.

I truly appreciate all of your return phone calls, but mostly the ones where you just call to check on my progress. Though you're 3,000 miles away you successfully bridge that gap with the phone and fax.

My twenty year-old Subzero died last night and I take that as a sure sign that I need to pressure everyone to get this job moving. Although the demolition and remodel will have it's own sources of aggravation, I am entering into it calmly, knowing that you'll help me see the light through the headaches and decisions that will come up.

It has been a pleasure working with you thus far and I look forward to continue to learn from you as the project moves forward and even as I remove hot foods from my new oven. I can hardly wait.

Sincerely,
Ellen Fuss

Donald E. Silvers
Kitchens and Other Environments By Design

Dear Don,

We are at last happily ensconced in our beautiful new kitchen! And it's everything you promised it would be: warm, lovely, efficient and only half-again our original budget. Of course, we knew when we started that we would have to pay for the quality that we wanted. The scary part was whether or not we would get what we wanted and whether we would be speaking to anybody by the time we finished. This is just to let you know that we are very happy with the kitchen, with you, with Doug Carlson, and with each other!

Unlike our other remodeling projects, this one seemed to go off with very few hitches. And the planning process was really fun. I must confess, I had initial concerns that our ideas might not mesh, but I soon found that you listened well and figured out what I wanted better than I did! Thank you for your gentle encouragement and/or discouragement of the myriad decisions we had to make. Yes, the double chef's sink is great; Yes, I'm glad I stuck to my guns about the dishwasher placement; Yes, Delta turned out to be the best deal for the hood; Yes, a dark floor is best (and to my surprise, friends have really admired it), etc. We love how everything works together visually - especially my special order tile. Congratulations! Your design sense me my chicken challenge and triumphed!

As far as how it all works as a kitchen, it's coming together quite nicely. I still turn the wrong way out of habit to reach for things, but the good news is that everything is only a step or two away in another direction. I keep forgetting to use the new prep sink but when I really need it, I'm sure glad it's there. I'm not sure I have quite as much storage space (although I haven't finished moving things around) but at least I've finally tossed out a lot of old, unused stuff. Nostalgia be damned! Now, about those old pots and pans...

I think my only complaint, which we have discussed before, is the cupboard depth. Between you and Doug and Earl, I wish someone had warned us that these 12 inch cabinets had only 11 inches of usable depth inside. I never thought that these 12 inch cabinets had only 11 inches of usable depth inside. I never thought that a mere inch could cause such frustration! At least things were modified adequately and promptly. We've been very happy with Highcastle and Doug, too. You all make a good team.

Thank you for making this remodel such an educational and enjoyable process. George and I have much enjoyed getting to know you and work with you. Though we seem to be out of projects, we hope we can stay in touch well after our pending inaugural dinner.

Sincerely,
Laurie
Stoneman

Mr. Don Silvers Kitchen by design
155 S. Orange Drive
Los Angeles, CA 90036

Dear Don,

Thought I'd drop you a line to let you know how pleased I am with the kitchen you designed for me.

The most amazing thing is I can literally stand in one place and prepare a whole meal from salad or soup to dessert. My freezer, refrigerator, oven, stove, and utensils are at an arms reach and everything looks great, too.

One of my criteria was to bring as much of the outside inside. And you were extremely successful with this. The great room you designed for me is much lighter and brighter and a perfect gathering place for my large family.

I also have to mention how successful you were in structuring the space to give me a dining room to seat 16 people. Friends comment constantly on the impressiveness of the room and especially on the lighting and the coffered ceiling.

Best of all was your follow through and the thoroughness of your search for just the perfect tile or flooring or appliance to suit my cooking needs and preferences.

From our very first meeting, I felt I was in good hands and was never disappointed. You are a man who takes tremendous pride in your work and it shows in the dozens of kitchens you've designed.

Sincerely,
Shelley D. Leow

2410 Nichols Canyon Road
Los Angeles, CA 90046
August 19, 1997

Don Silvers
155 S. Orange Drive
Los Angeles CA 90036

Dear Don:

From the moment Lucy and I moved into our house, I knew that the kitchen would have to be remodeled. It was a kitchen that had obviously been designed by an architect who had never actually cooked. I was therefore delighted when I stumbled across your lecture at the Pacific Design Center about designing a kitchen with cooking in mind. Five minutes into the lecture, I knew that you were the person to assist me in realizing my dream kitchen.

I have immensely enjoyed working with you on the design and in particular appreciated:

• The fact that you don't sell anything other than your expertise.
• Your strong opinions on what works and doesn't work in a kitchen coupled with your willingess to explain the principles underlying your design recommendations.

• Your unusual first step of inviting the client to watch you cook dinner in your own kitchen. I must admit that I was skeptical at first but quickly changed my mind once I realized that seeing you cook caused me to question many of the assumptions I had made about what I wanted for my kitchen.

• Your willingness to obsess with me about the details, including the numerous design meetings, countless trips to tile stores and appliance and cabinet showrooms, and the continuing consultations throughout the actual construction.

Although today, as I sit amidst the sawdust, plaster, and general mayhem and I vow that I will never again go through another remodel in my life, I actually secretly hope that I will someday move into another house with a deficient kitchen so I can call on your services once again.

Sincerely,
Rob Biniaz

To Whom It may Concern:

I am a avid cook and lover of all things in a kitchen. Several years ago, I had the opportunity to remodel our kitchen. It began as a research project. However, the more I researched, the more questions I had.

I was referred to Don Silvers, who was in the process of working with some friends of mine remodeling their kitchen. I was skeptical of the very concept of a "kitchen designer." After all, it was a working kitchen with all the professional equipment and accouterments that I was after, not just a pretty "designer" kitchen.

Wrong, wrong, wrong...I was wrong. Don helped teach me what a kitchen could be, and he did this in a very logical and professional way. I thought I knew about kitchen equipment and toys. Don was at a different level. He helped me decide what I needed and why. I learned that equipment isn't just equipment; it truly depends on one's needs. I even think differently about how I organize items in the kitchen——from the pantry to the refrigerator——to maximize efficiency and minimize upkeep.

The results far exceeded my expectations, and I also ended up with a beautiful "designer" kitchen. I have just completed my second Don Silvers kitchen——we moved. As a truly fitting testimonial, I can honestly and happily say that there is nothing I would change——both times. They actually improve!

Sincerely,
Randy Katz

In the next several pages are a dozen kitchens that I have designed. All of them follow the concepts in the book you are reading. All of them have been designed for the client based on their needs and their desire as to how their kitchen should look.

Ambiance is very personal – you the reader may or may not like how a kitchen looks - it's not relevant whether you do or you don't, because the client loves it and that's what was important.

On the functional side, they all perform in the same manner with lots of counter space where needed, and storage where needed. Point of use is prevalent throughout the entire dozen kitchens.

Kitchen number I is my daughter's kitchen. Her question was "Can we make it better without remodeling?" As you look at her kitchen, notice the left side – I added a sink to the existing counter. That took the kitchen from a one cook kitchen to three or more.

In conclusion, my kitchen, number XI, and that of our downstairs neighbors, number X, are the exact same space but as you can see two totally different kitchens. They have the same layouts but serve two different styles of cooking, so as you could see beautiful kitchens cook beautifully.

The contractors, plumbers, electricians, rough & finished framers, cabinet and appliance salespeople are all involved in helping me create the kitchens I've designed. I want to say thank you to each one of you.

Client List of Kitchens

I. Michelle & Eric De Beus

II. Robert Seale

III. Blanche & Neal Ames

IV. Cori & Dick Lowe

V. Cecila Dan

VI. Jessica & Arlan Cohen

VII. Maureen & Bob Lucas

VIII. Randy & Kathy Katz

IV. Kathy & John Hanson

X. Sue & Chris Thalkin

XI. Sally & Don Silvers

XII. Mary & Brian Buchanan

CLEAN-UP

PREP

CLEAN-UP

PREP

II

CLEAN-UP

PREP

III

PREP

CLEAN-UP

PREP

CLEAN-UP

V

PREP

CLEAN-UP

VI

CLEAN-UP

PREP

VII

PREP

CLEAN-UP

VIII

CLEAN-UP

PREP

IX

CLEAN-UP

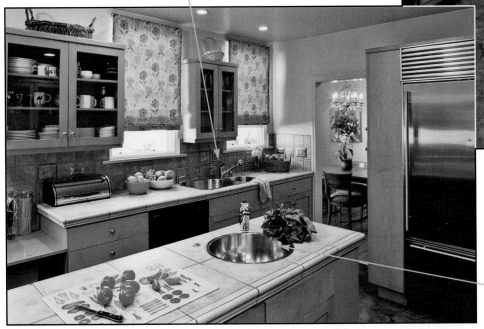

PREP

X